HOW IT WORKS

THE WORLD'S
WEATHER

Michael Allaby

HORUS EDITIONS

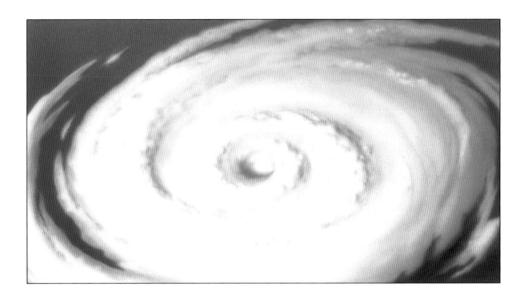

Published by Horus Editions
Award Publications Limited,
1st Floor, 27 Longford Street,
London NW1 3DZ

Copyright © 2002 Horus Editions

Series editor Elizabeth Miles
Designed by Steve Weston, Richard Rowan
Illustrations by David Draper, Martin Sanders, Mike Saunders,
Jim Channell

ISBN 1-899762-54-X

Printed in Singapore

HOW IT WORKS
CONTENTS

The Sun's Power

THE SUN is a star. Like other stars it is a huge ball of fire. We can see by the light from that fire and we can feel its warmth. If the Sun was not there, the Earth would be a bitterly cold, dark, dead place.

Earth lies beneath a blanket of gases. We call the mixture of gases 'air'. The entire blanket is the atmosphere. Some of the radiation (energy) that reaches Earth from the Sun is absorbed near the top of the atmosphere, but most passes through the air all the way to the surface of the land and sea. Some is reflected by bright clouds, snow, and other light colours. The rest is absorbed, warming the ground and the water. When land and sea are warmed they in turn warm the air next to them. The warm air rises, and this movement of air results in the weather.

Trapped

The Sun emits particles. Some are trapped by a force called the Earth's magnetism. They are swept down and around the North and South Poles. They shine when they collide with atoms of oxygen and nitrogen in the air. This makes the northern and southern lights, or aurorae. Like curtains of light they ripple, more than 300 kilometres above our heads.

AURORA

A SMALL AMOUNT OF SUNLIGHT IS ABSORBED HIGH IN THE ATMOSPHERE

IN THE STRATOSPHERE OXYGEN ABSORBS ULTRAVIOLET (UV) RADIATION FROM THE SUN, FORMING OZONE, WHICH ALSO ABSORBS UV

SUNLIGHT IS REFLECTED BY CLOUDS

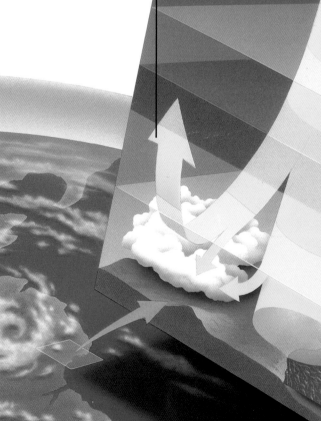

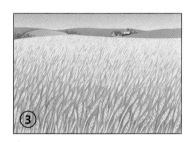

Reflected

All surfaces reflect some of the sunlight falling on them. Bare soil exposed when forest trees are felled (1) reflects about 25 per cent. A forest (2) reflects about 15 per cent.

Conifer (pine) forests reflect less than broad-leaved forests because they are darker. A field of wheat (3) reflects about 20 per cent, while fresh snow on a mountainside reflects about 90 per cent (4).

THERE IS NO CLEAR TOP TO THE ATMOSPHERE, THE AIR JUST GETS THINNER

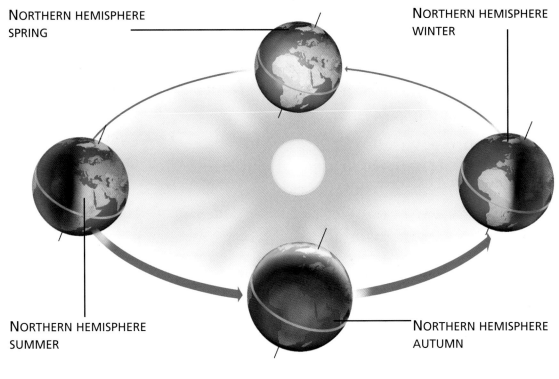

NORTHERN HEMISPHERE SPRING

NORTHERN HEMISPHERE WINTER

NORTHERN HEMISPHERE SUMMER

NORTHERN HEMISPHERE AUTUMN

The four seasons
The Earth turns on its axis, but the axis is not vertical. This means that as the Earth moves around the Sun, first one half is tilted towards the Sun, and then the other. It is summer in the half facing the Sun and winter in the other half. In spring and autumn the Sun shines on both halves equally.

THE MESOSPHERE ENDS AT ABOUT 80 KILOMETRES

THE BOUNDARY AT THE BOTTOM OF THE MESOSPHERE IS CALLED THE STRATOPAUSE

OZONE IS CONCENTRATED IN THE OZONE LAYER – IT HELPS TO PROTECT US FROM THE SUN'S UV RAYS

THE GROUND ALSO RADIATES WARMTH INTO THE AIR

WE INHABIT THE TROPOSPHERE

Atmosphere
The atmosphere extends to about 1000 kilometres above the Earth, but 99.9 per cent of the air is in the lowest 50 kilometres. Above about 6 kilometres there is not enough air to breathe.

As you climb, the temperature falls. It goes on falling to about 12 kilometres where it is about –60 °C. Then it remains the same. This height marks the boundary, called the tropopause, between the troposphere below and the stratosphere above. Weather happens in the troposphere.

Above about 20 kilometres the temperature starts to rise again. This is because oxygen is absorbing ultraviolet (UV) radiation from the Sun and forming ozone. Absorbing radiation heats the air.

The stratosphere ends at the stratopause, about 50 kilometres above the Earth's surface. Beyond that lies the mesosphere, where the temperature decreases as you climb. It ends at the mesopause, at about 80 kilometres. Above the mesopause, the thermosphere merges gradually with space.

Climates

THE PRAIRIES of North America (*see right*, 1) and steppes of Eurasia (2) are vast grassland areas. Go to the centre of Brazil (3) and you will find the land blanketed with tropical rain forest. Most of North Africa (4) and the Arabian Peninsula (5) is desert. Each of these types of vegetation is different and each is typical of a particular type of climate that covers a large part of the world.

Climate is the pattern of weather recorded at a place over a long period of time. Every part of the world has its own climate. Each climate is associated with certain kinds of plants and the animals that live among those plants. Climates are often classified (grouped together) according to the type of vegetation or farming they support.

Continental grasslands
Bison have thick coats that keep them warm in the bitterly cold winters on the North American prairie. The grasses of the prairie, the South American pampas, and Eurasian steppe grow well in the dry continental climates.

Polar climates
Polar bears spend much of their time on the arctic ice that surrounds the North Pole. They have thick coats, and fur on the soles of their feet. Tundra vegetation (grasses, sedges, rushes, and small bushes) grows around the edge of the arctic.

Tropical forest
Tropical forests grow where the weather is always warm. Some places have rain all year, in others it is seasonal.

Continents
In continents, far from the ocean, the climate is fairly dry. Summers are often very hot and winters very cold.

Desert
It seldom rains in a desert. Some deserts are hot, but those in Central Asia and Argentina are often cold.

Polar
Temperatures are below freezing most or all of the year. In Antarctica and central Greenland the weather is very dry.

Temperate
These regions are rarely very hot or cold. Rainfall is moderate – in some places seasonal, in others falling all year.

Highland
Temperature decreases with height. This means a mountain climate can be tropical at the foot and polar at the summit.

Temperate climate
The mild winters, warm summers, and rain throughout the year, plus the dry, sunny spells to ripen grain, make this an ideal climate for growing crops and raising cattle on pasture.

Highland
Many mountain plants and animals live at only one level, but deer, sheep, and goats feed on high pastures in summer and move lower down in winter. The agile mountain lion, or puma, follows them.

② ④ ⑤

Desert
The dromedary (camel) thrives in the dry, hot desert. Its body does not overheat and it can survive for long periods without food or water.

Tropical forest
Constant warmth and lots of rain produce the giant trees and other plants of the tropical rain forests. There is plenty to eat for tree-dwellers such as South American spider monkeys.

Wind Machine

WIND is moving air. Air moves because there is less of it in some places than in others. When air is warm it expands. Its molecules move further apart, so they occupy more space and the air becomes less dense. Cold air is denser. Its molecules crowd closer together so there are more of them in any given space. Air flows from where it is dense to where the molecules are less crowded – a little like air rushing out of a bike tyre when you remove the valve.

If the Sun heated the Earth evenly, and the land and sea were warmed and cooled equally everywhere, there would be no wind. But this is not what happens. Some places are warmer than others and so air is denser in some places. Winds help distribute the Sun's warmth. They carry warm air into cold places and cold air into warm places.

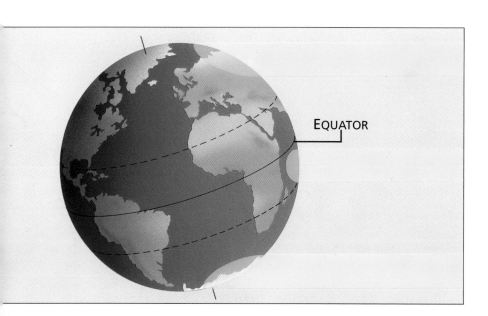

EQUATOR

Trade winds

Trade winds are the most reliable winds on Earth. They blow towards the equator, from the northeast in the northern hemisphere and from the southeast in the southern hemisphere. Where they meet, the air rises and huge rain clouds form. The air descends again and flows back towards the equator, and so produces the trade winds.

ONE OF TWO JET STREAMS IN THE NORTHERN HEMISPHERE

PARTS OF THE GLOBAL WIND SYSTEM FLOW IN CIRCULAR PATTERNS, CALLED CELLS – THIS IS THE MID-LATITUDE FERREL CELL

DRY, WARM AIR SINKS

WARM, MOIST AIR RISES, THEN MOVES AWAY FROM THE EQUATOR

THE EQUATOR DIVIDES THE GLOBE

THE EARTH TURNS FROM WEST TO EAST, MAKING THE WINDS CURVE

THIS VERTICAL MOVEMENT OF TROPICAL AIR IS CALLED A HADLEY CELL

COLD, DENSE AIR SINKS OVER THE POLES, THEN FLOWS AWAY FROM THE POLAR REGIONS

COLD AIR FLOWING SOUTH MEETS WARM AIR FLOWING NORTH, AND THE AIR RISES

AIR RISES IN THE FERREL CELL WHERE COLD, POLAR AIR MEETS WARMER AIR FROM MIDDLE LATITUDES

Sun's rays

Near the equator the Sun is almost directly overhead at noon. It shines very intensely because its rays are concentrated. Near the Arctic and Antarctica the Sun is low in the sky, even in summer. Its rays are less intense because they are spread over a bigger area. That is why it is warmer at the equator than near the North and South Poles.

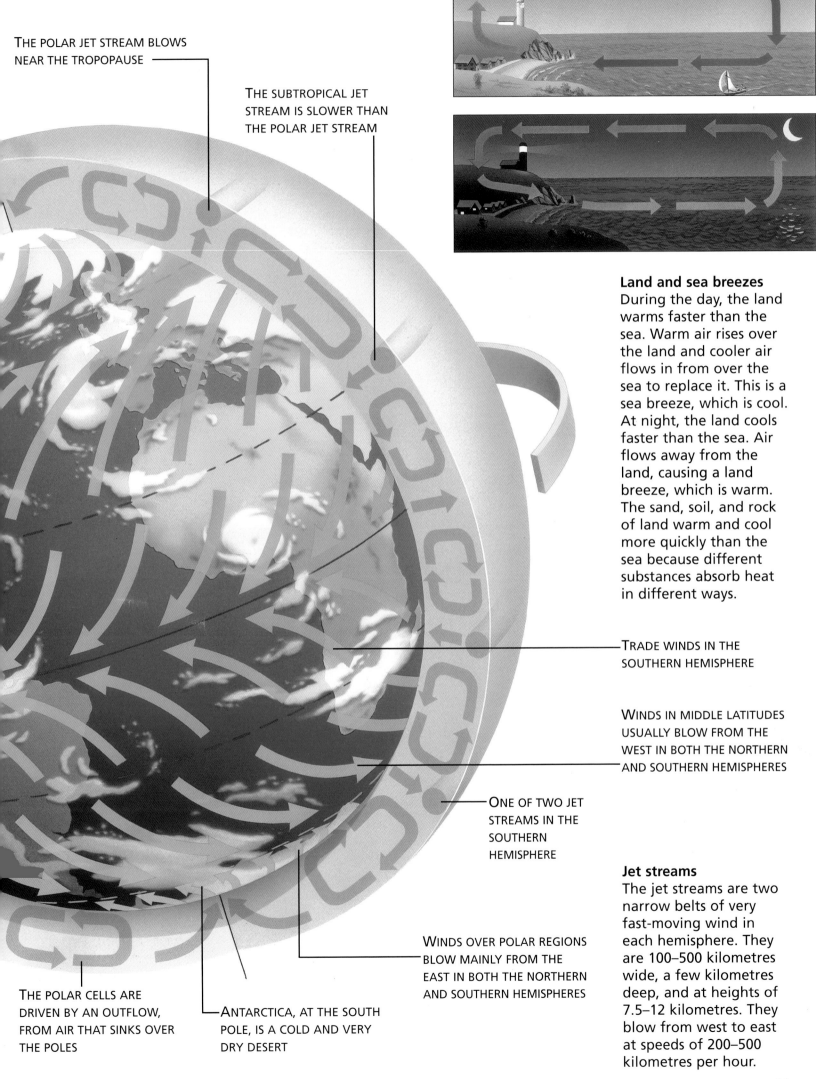

THE POLAR JET STREAM BLOWS NEAR THE TROPOPAUSE

THE SUBTROPICAL JET STREAM IS SLOWER THAN THE POLAR JET STREAM

Land and sea breezes

During the day, the land warms faster than the sea. Warm air rises over the land and cooler air flows in from over the sea to replace it. This is a sea breeze, which is cool. At night, the land cools faster than the sea. Air flows away from the land, causing a land breeze, which is warm. The sand, soil, and rock of land warm and cool more quickly than the sea because different substances absorb heat in different ways.

TRADE WINDS IN THE SOUTHERN HEMISPHERE

WINDS IN MIDDLE LATITUDES USUALLY BLOW FROM THE WEST IN BOTH THE NORTHERN AND SOUTHERN HEMISPHERES

ONE OF TWO JET STREAMS IN THE SOUTHERN HEMISPHERE

Jet streams

The jet streams are two narrow belts of very fast-moving wind in each hemisphere. They are 100–500 kilometres wide, a few kilometres deep, and at heights of 7.5–12 kilometres. They blow from west to east at speeds of 200–500 kilometres per hour.

WINDS OVER POLAR REGIONS BLOW MAINLY FROM THE EAST IN BOTH THE NORTHERN AND SOUTHERN HEMISPHERES

THE POLAR CELLS ARE DRIVEN BY AN OUTFLOW, FROM AIR THAT SINKS OVER THE POLES

ANTARCTICA, AT THE SOUTH POLE, IS A COLD AND VERY DRY DESERT

Water World

WATER covers more than 70 per cent of the Earth's surface, but most of it is seawater. Only 3 per cent is fresh water, which land-dwelling plants and animals can use, and 75 per cent of that is in polar regions and permanently frozen. Water reaches the land as fog, dew, hail, rain, and snow. It is fresh because when seawater evaporates (turns into a gas), its salt is left behind in the sea.

When water in the sea, lakes, rivers, and ground is heated by the Sun and evaporates, it becomes airborne water vapour. It then cools and condenses (turns into water droplets) to form dew, fog, and clouds. At ground-level some evaporates again, while the rest drains into rivers that carry it back to the sea. Water is always circulating, from sea to land and back again. This is called the water, or hydrological, cycle.

Rainbows
A rainbow appears when light is bent and reflected inside rain-drops. The different colours of light are bent by different amounts, so they appear separately.

WHEN AIR RISES AND COOLS, THE AIRBORNE WATER VAPOUR CONDENSES TO FORM CLOUDS

WATER THAT EVAPORATES FROM THE SEA IS CARRIED OVER THE LAND BY WINDS

Water vapour
Water vapour is a gas. Even the driest air contains some water vapour. You cannot see it, smell it, or taste it. It consists of water molecules moving in all directions.

WHEN HEATED, WATER FROM THE SEA EVAPORATES AND ENTERS THE AIR

WATER VAPOUR MOLECULES ARE SEPARATE – EACH HAS TWO HYDROGEN ATOMS AND ONE OXYGEN ATOM

HYDROGEN ATOM   OXYGEN ATOM

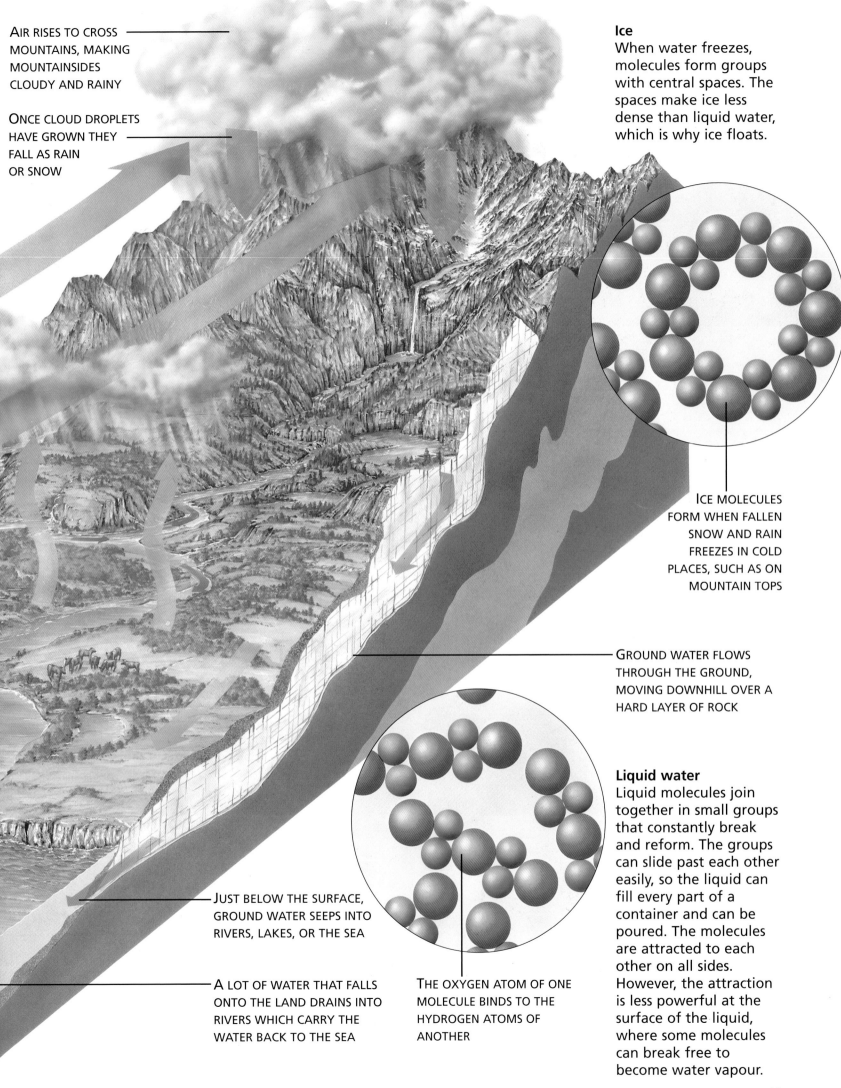

AIR RISES TO CROSS MOUNTAINS, MAKING MOUNTAINSIDES CLOUDY AND RAINY

ONCE CLOUD DROPLETS HAVE GROWN THEY FALL AS RAIN OR SNOW

Ice
When water freezes, molecules form groups with central spaces. The spaces make ice less dense than liquid water, which is why ice floats.

ICE MOLECULES FORM WHEN FALLEN SNOW AND RAIN FREEZES IN COLD PLACES, SUCH AS ON MOUNTAIN TOPS

GROUND WATER FLOWS THROUGH THE GROUND, MOVING DOWNHILL OVER A HARD LAYER OF ROCK

JUST BELOW THE SURFACE, GROUND WATER SEEPS INTO RIVERS, LAKES, OR THE SEA

Liquid water
Liquid molecules join together in small groups that constantly break and reform. The groups can slide past each other easily, so the liquid can fill every part of a container and can be poured. The molecules are attracted to each other on all sides. However, the attraction is less powerful at the surface of the liquid, where some molecules can break free to become water vapour.

A LOT OF WATER THAT FALLS ONTO THE LAND DRAINS INTO RIVERS WHICH CARRY THE WATER BACK TO THE SEA

THE OXYGEN ATOM OF ONE MOLECULE BINDS TO THE HYDROGEN ATOMS OF ANOTHER

Clouds

WARM AIR can hold more water vapour than cold air can. If warm air cools down, it will not be able to hold as much water vapour as it did, and some of its moisture may condense into liquid droplets. You can see this happen when the moisture in your warm breath condenses on a cold window.

Air temperature decreases with height. So, as air rises it also becomes cooler. If the rising air is moist some of its water vapour may condense into tiny water droplets that hang in the air. Clouds are made up from many millions of these droplets. Clouds vary – some are flat and smooth, others are fluffy, some are huge and black. These differences are due to the speed at which the air rises. Smooth sheets of cloud form in air that is rising slowly. Storm clouds grow in air that is rising very fast.

High-level clouds
These clouds form more than 6000 metres above the surface, where the air is very cold. The clouds are white and thin, wispy or feathery. They are made from tiny ice crystals.

CIRRUS CLOUD FORMS WISPY STRANDS

Mid-level clouds
Clouds that form at heights of 2000 to 6000 metres have names beginning with 'alto', in fact meaning 'high'. They are made from water droplets. Light rain or snow can fall from them.

ALTOCUMULUS FORMS SMALL, ROUND PATCHES OR ROLLS OF CLOUD THAT SOMETIMES MERGE

ALTOSTRATUS IS A SMOOTH GREY CLOUD THAT JUST ALLOWS THE SUN TO SHOW AS A GLOW

④

STRATOCUMULUS ARE PATCHES OR ROLLS OF LOW-LEVEL CLOUD MADE FROM WATER DROPLETS

Rising air
Air can rise for different reasons, for example convection (*above, left*). Here, warm land and sea heat the air next to them. This makes the air expand, so it is less dense. Cooler, denser air sinks and pushes the warm air up. Then the cool air is warmed and the process goes on. Orographic lifting ('orographic' means to do with mountains) happens when surface air meets a mountain range and is forced to rise (*centre*). When warm and cold air meet at a front (*right*), they do not mix. Instead, the warm air rises over the cold air.

Vapour trails

Long streams of cloud sometimes stretch out from an aircraft. The hot exhaust from the engines contains water vapour. The exhaust cools rapidly in the cold air and the water vapour changes directly into crystals of ice.

Cumulonimbus

These are dark, thick clouds that bring heavy showers of rain, snow or hail. Big cumulonimbus clouds (1) cause thunderstorms and they can produce tornadoes. The cloud base is near the ground but the top of the cloud is often at a height of more than 12 kilometres.

Lower-level clouds

Dull, grey clouds that form below 2000 metres often cover the sky. Their names include 'strat', meaning layer. Stratus is flat, grey low cloud. Nimbostratus (2) is the cloud that is the main cause of light drizzle, rain, and snow.

Banner cloud stretches downwind from a mountain peak (3). Cooling towers can create low-level clouds (4). Water used for cooling vaporizes and then condenses above the towers.

CUMULUS CLOUD IS SEPARATE PATCHES OF WHITE, FLUFFY CLOUD THAT OFTEN FORM IN FINE WEATHER

Highs and Lows

AIR FROM THE JET STREAM SINKS TO PRODUCE HIGH PRESSURE NEAR THE GROUND

WHEN THERE IS HIGH PRESSURE NEAR THE GROUND, THERE IS LOW PRESSURE IN THE UPPER AIR

JET STREAM

A COLD FRONT

AN AREA OF HIGH PRESSURE

THE HIGHER THE PRESSURE AT THE CENTRE, THE STRONGER THE WINDS

AIR EXPANDS when it grows warmer. Its molecules move further apart and so the air becomes less dense. A column of warm air reaching up from the ground contains fewer molecules than a similar column of cold air, so the warm air weighs less and exerts less pressure. It forms an area of low pressure. If the air is cold the opposite happens. Its molecules move closer together, its density increases, and it forms an area of high pressure.

Air moves towards areas of low pressure and away from areas of high pressure. The Earth's rotation then makes the air flow around the areas of high and low pressure.

Warm air and cool air do not mix easily. A boundary, called a front, forms between them. Areas of high and low pressure, and the fronts separating them, produce our weather.

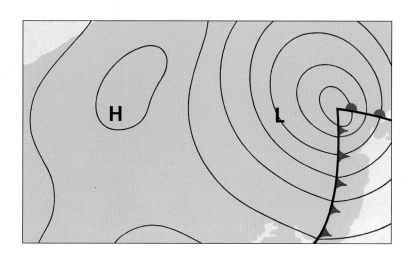

Weather chart
The lines on a weather chart are called isobars. They join places where the pressure is the same. Their patterns reveal centres of high (H) and low (L) pressure. Winds blow roughly parallel to the isobars. Fronts are shown by lines across the isobars. Semicircles indicate a warm front, with warm air behind it. Triangles mark a cold front. Where they meet, cold air is moving beneath warm air and lifting it from the ground. This produces a centre of low pressure called a depression.

High pressure
High pressure often means fine weather. Air is sinking and flowing outwards. Surface air flows clockwise around a centre of high pressure in the northern hemisphere and anti-clockwise in the southern. An area of high pressure is also called an anticyclone.

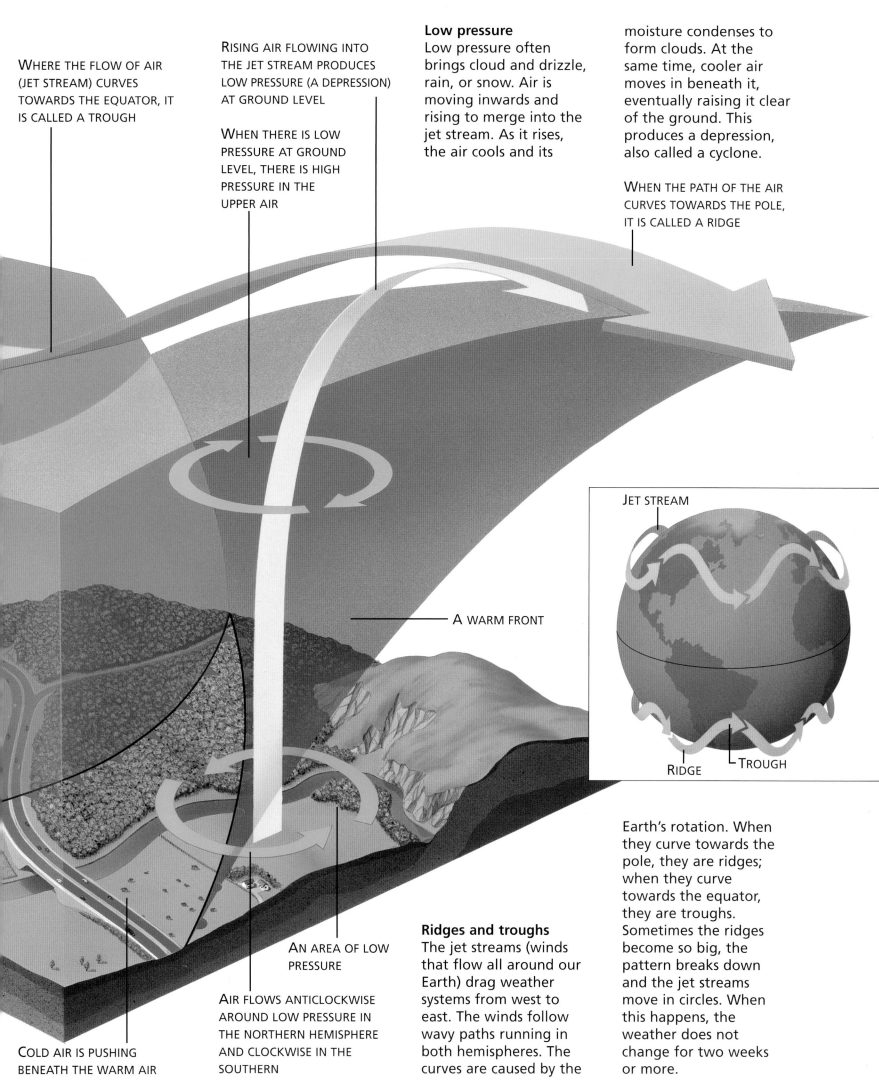

WHERE THE FLOW OF AIR (JET STREAM) CURVES TOWARDS THE EQUATOR, IT IS CALLED A TROUGH

RISING AIR FLOWING INTO THE JET STREAM PRODUCES LOW PRESSURE (A DEPRESSION) AT GROUND LEVEL

WHEN THERE IS LOW PRESSURE AT GROUND LEVEL, THERE IS HIGH PRESSURE IN THE UPPER AIR

Low pressure
Low pressure often brings cloud and drizzle, rain, or snow. Air is moving inwards and rising to merge into the jet stream. As it rises, the air cools and its

moisture condenses to form clouds. At the same time, cooler air moves in beneath it, eventually raising it clear of the ground. This produces a depression, also called a cyclone.

WHEN THE PATH OF THE AIR CURVES TOWARDS THE POLE, IT IS CALLED A RIDGE

A WARM FRONT

JET STREAM

RIDGE   TROUGH

AN AREA OF LOW PRESSURE

COLD AIR IS PUSHING BENEATH THE WARM AIR

AIR FLOWS ANTICLOCKWISE AROUND LOW PRESSURE IN THE NORTHERN HEMISPHERE AND CLOCKWISE IN THE SOUTHERN

Ridges and troughs
The jet streams (winds that flow all around our Earth) drag weather systems from west to east. The winds follow wavy paths running in both hemispheres. The curves are caused by the

Earth's rotation. When they curve towards the pole, they are ridges; when they curve towards the equator, they are troughs. Sometimes the ridges become so big, the pattern breaks down and the jet streams move in circles. When this happens, the weather does not change for two weeks or more.

Fronts

COLD AIR is denser than warm air. When the two meet, instead of mixing together, the cold, dense air pushes under the warm air or the warm air rides over the cold air. Eventually, all of the warm air is raised clear of the ground.

The boundary where warm and cold air meet is called a front. If the air behind a moving front is cooler than the air ahead, it is a cold front. If the air behind the front is warmer, it is a warm front. 'Warm' and 'cold' mean only that one mass of air is warm or cool compared with the other.

When the warm air begins to be lifted clear of the surface, the cold and warm fronts are said to be occluded, or to 'form an occlusion'. Once they have occluded, both of the fronts slowly disappear.

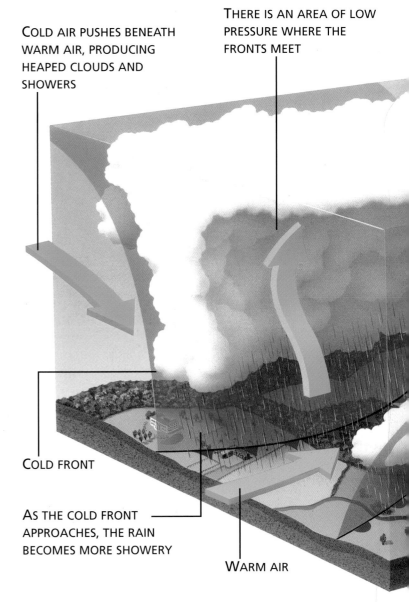

COLD AIR PUSHES BENEATH WARM AIR, PRODUCING HEAPED CLOUDS AND SHOWERS

THERE IS AN AREA OF LOW PRESSURE WHERE THE FRONTS MEET

COLD FRONT

AS THE COLD FRONT APPROACHES, THE RAIN BECOMES MORE SHOWERY

WARM AIR

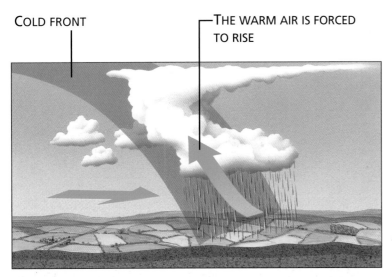

COLD FRONT

THE WARM AIR IS FORCED TO RISE

Cold front

A cold front is at the leading edge of a mass of cold air (see *left*). It pushes under the warmer air like a wedge. As the warmer air rises heaped clouds form, often bringing rain or snow. Because of the slope, clouds along the front are in the warmer air that lies above the colder air. Small, puffy clouds appear lower down in the sky when the front is moving away.

Warm front

The warm front slopes more gently than the cold front. Warm air is pushed quite slowly up the front (see *left*). Its water vapour condenses to form sheets of cloud.

The lower clouds often bring light but fairly continuous rain, drizzle, or snow. The cloud sometimes extends a long way into the warm air behind the front, which can mean several days of dull, wet weather.

Because of the slope, cloud also extends a long way ahead of the front. When the first wisps of thin cloud appear high overhead, the place where the front touches the ground is still about 400 kilometres away.

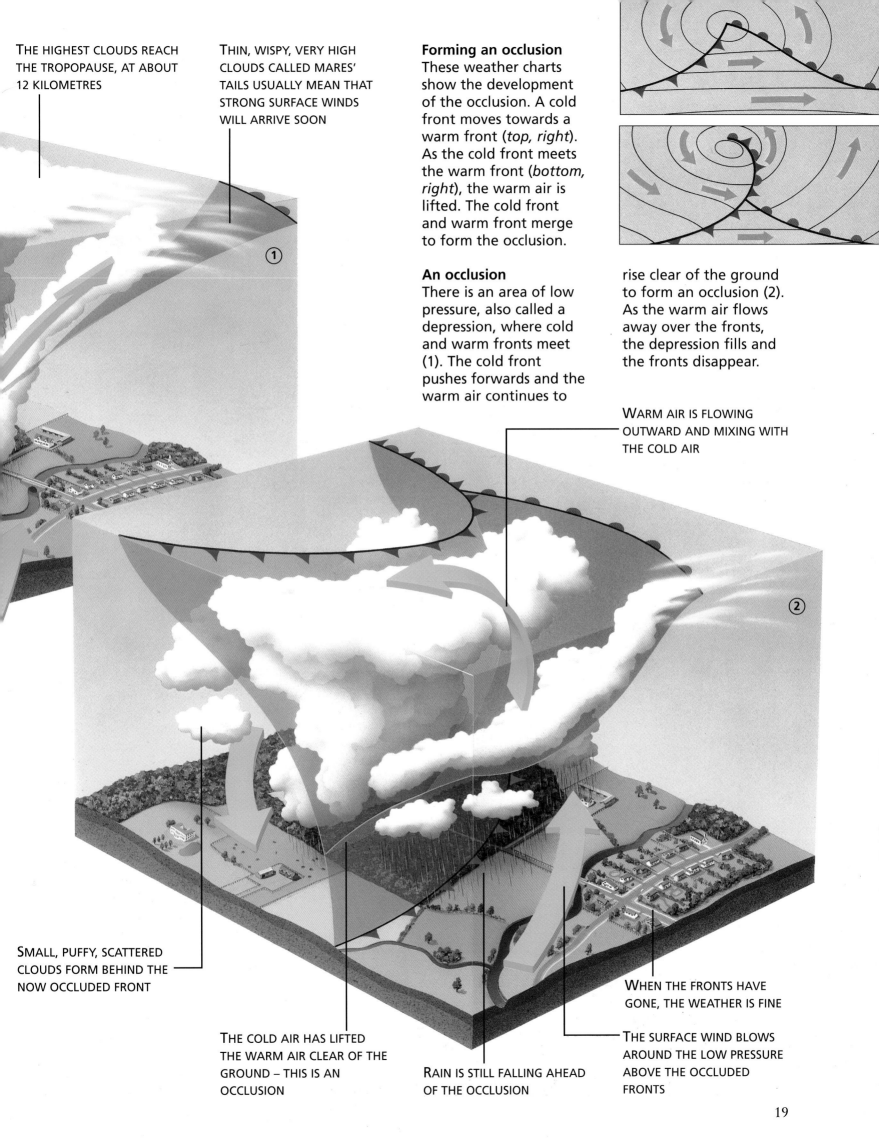

THE HIGHEST CLOUDS REACH THE TROPOPAUSE, AT ABOUT 12 KILOMETRES

THIN, WISPY, VERY HIGH CLOUDS CALLED MARES' TAILS USUALLY MEAN THAT STRONG SURFACE WINDS WILL ARRIVE SOON

Forming an occlusion
These weather charts show the development of the occlusion. A cold front moves towards a warm front (*top, right*). As the cold front meets the warm front (*bottom, right*), the warm air is lifted. The cold front and warm front merge to form the occlusion.

An occlusion
There is an area of low pressure, also called a depression, where cold and warm fronts meet (1). The cold front pushes forwards and the warm air continues to rise clear of the ground to form an occlusion (2). As the warm air flows away over the fronts, the depression fills and the fronts disappear.

WARM AIR IS FLOWING OUTWARD AND MIXING WITH THE COLD AIR

SMALL, PUFFY, SCATTERED CLOUDS FORM BEHIND THE NOW OCCLUDED FRONT

THE COLD AIR HAS LIFTED THE WARM AIR CLEAR OF THE GROUND – THIS IS AN OCCLUSION

RAIN IS STILL FALLING AHEAD OF THE OCCLUSION

WHEN THE FRONTS HAVE GONE, THE WEATHER IS FINE

THE SURFACE WIND BLOWS AROUND THE LOW PRESSURE ABOVE THE OCCLUDED FRONTS

Rain and Snow

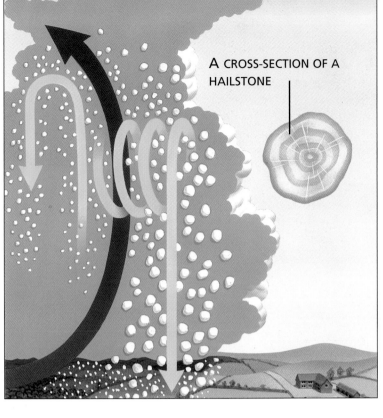

A CROSS-SECTION OF A HAILSTONE

WARM AIR can hold more water vapour than cold air can. As moist air cools, some of its water vapour condenses into liquid droplets. These form clouds. The droplets are so tiny that they only fall very slowly. When they reach drier air they evaporate, but more vapour condenses to replace them. In large clouds the droplets can grow. They may merge together or freeze into ice crystals that stick together, making snowflakes. As they grow bigger and heavier, they fall faster. Eventually, they fall out of the cloud. If they reach the ground they are called drizzle, rain, or snow.

Outside the tropics most rain consists of snowflakes that have melted in warm air. We only see snow if the air between the cloud and ground is below freezing.

Hailstones
In storm clouds, pieces of ice are lifted to the top, covered with cold water as they fall, then lifted high enough to freeze again. This is how hailstones grow, layer by layer (see *above*).

ABOVE THIS LEVEL THE TEMPERATURE IS BELOW FREEZING

Tropical rain
In the tropics (places on and near the equator) the hot sunshine makes air rise fast and because it is so warm the air carries a lot of moisture. As the air rises and cools, the moisture condenses into clouds which produce showers or heavy rain.

LARGE, HEAVY WATER DROPLETS QUICKLY FORM IN THE MOIST TROPICAL AIR

OUTSIDE THE TROPICS THE AIR IS COOLER

IN THE TROPICS, THE WATER DROPLETS DO NOT FREEZE

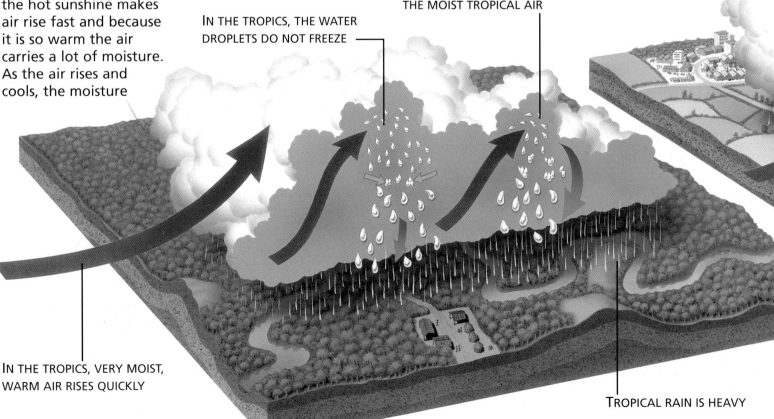

IN THE TROPICS, VERY MOIST, WARM AIR RISES QUICKLY

TROPICAL RAIN IS HEAVY

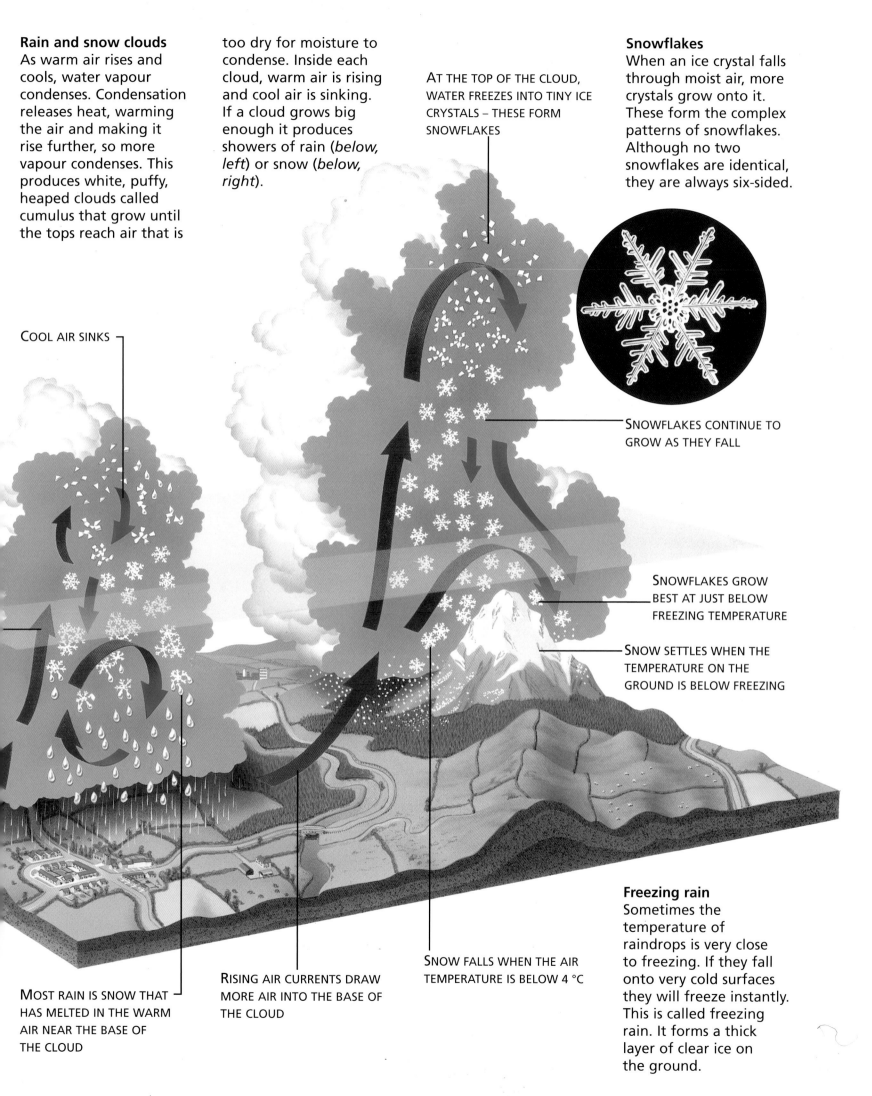

Rain and snow clouds
As warm air rises and cools, water vapour condenses. Condensation releases heat, warming the air and making it rise further, so more vapour condenses. This produces white, puffy, heaped clouds called cumulus that grow until the tops reach air that is too dry for moisture to condense. Inside each cloud, warm air is rising and cool air is sinking. If a cloud grows big enough it produces showers of rain (*below, left*) or snow (*below, right*).

AT THE TOP OF THE CLOUD, WATER FREEZES INTO TINY ICE CRYSTALS – THESE FORM SNOWFLAKES

Snowflakes
When an ice crystal falls through moist air, more crystals grow onto it. These form the complex patterns of snowflakes. Although no two snowflakes are identical, they are always six-sided.

COOL AIR SINKS

SNOWFLAKES CONTINUE TO GROW AS THEY FALL

SNOWFLAKES GROW BEST AT JUST BELOW FREEZING TEMPERATURE

SNOW SETTLES WHEN THE TEMPERATURE ON THE GROUND IS BELOW FREEZING

Freezing rain
Sometimes the temperature of raindrops is very close to freezing. If they fall onto very cold surfaces they will freeze instantly. This is called freezing rain. It forms a thick layer of clear ice on the ground.

SNOW FALLS WHEN THE AIR TEMPERATURE IS BELOW 4 °C

MOST RAIN IS SNOW THAT HAS MELTED IN THE WARM AIR NEAR THE BASE OF THE CLOUD

RISING AIR CURRENTS DRAW MORE AIR INTO THE BASE OF THE CLOUD

Thunderstorms

IF MOIST air rises fast enough, the condensation of its water vapour can build into a huge, black storm cloud, called a cumulonimbus. Inside the cloud, air is rising at about 160 kilometres per hour. Water is freezing near the top of the cloud and small pieces of ice are falling. The falling ice particles drag cold air behind them, so as well as the warm up-currents there are also cold down-currents.

The rising and falling ice particles become electrically charged. Quite soon, the upper part of the cloud has a positive charge and the lower part has a negative charge. The negative charge then produces a positive charge on the ground, beneath the cloud. When the difference in the charges is big enough, sparks fly between positive and negative. The sparks are what we see as lightning and hear as thunder.

WIND SWEEPS THE TOP OF THE CLOUD INTO AN ANVIL SHAPE

THE UPPER PART OF THE CLOUD HAS A POSITIVE CHARGE

AT THIS HEIGHT THERE ARE ONLY ICE CRYSTALS

UP-CURRENTS CARRY AIR AND MOISTURE ALL THE WAY TO THE TROPOPAUSE

THE HUGE CLOUD IS MADE UP OF ICE CRYSTALS AND WATER DROPLETS

Thunder
Lightning heats the air so strongly and so quickly that it explodes. Thunder is the sound of the exploding air. It rumbles because the noise takes longer to reach us from the top of the lightning stroke than it does from the bottom.

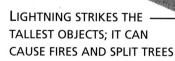

LIGHTNING STRIKES THE TALLEST OBJECTS; IT CAN CAUSE FIRES AND SPLIT TREES

All kinds of lightning
Lightning sparks occur between areas of positive and negative electrical charge. Lightning can flash between a cloud and the ground, or from one cloud to another, or between two parts of the same cloud. If it flashes to the ground (*above, left*) we see it as forked lightning. It may also appear as forked lightning if it flashes between clouds (*above, centre*), although flashes between clouds can also appear as sheet lightning. Lightning inside a cloud appears as a white flash of sheet lightning (*above, right*).

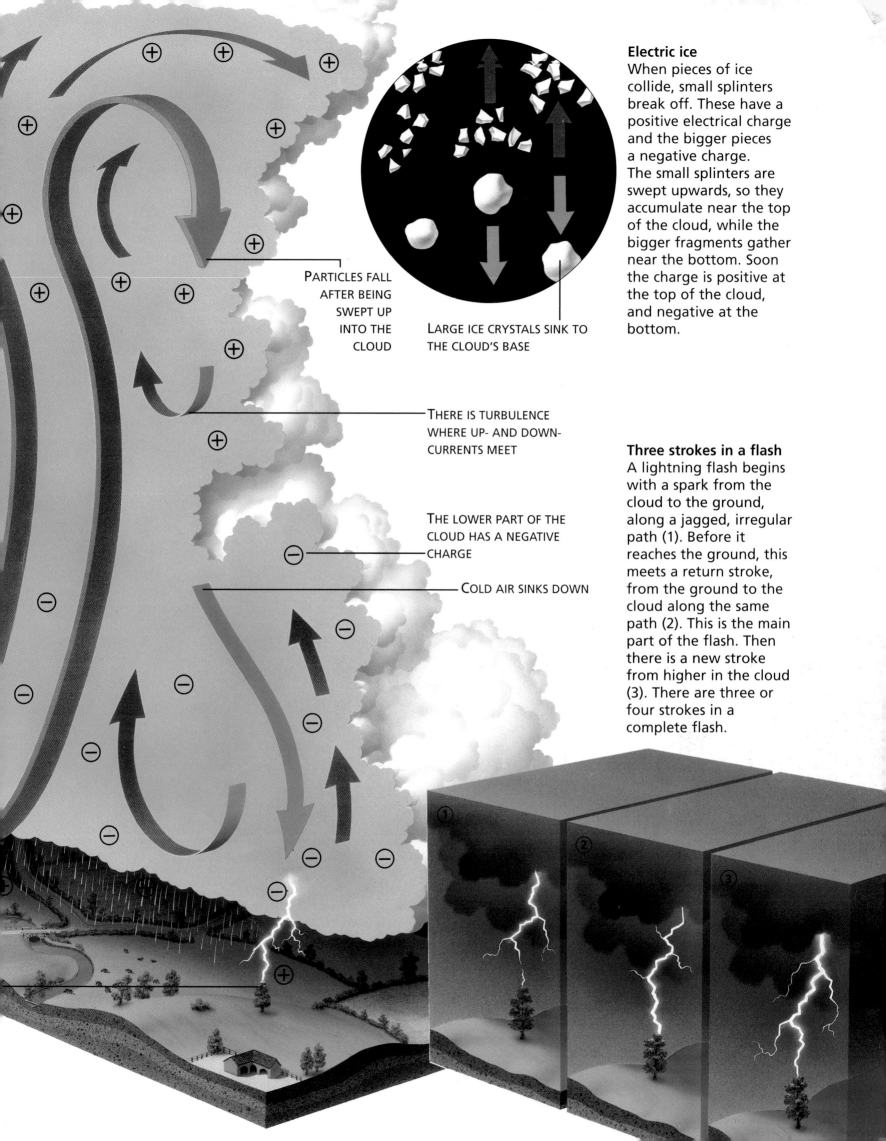

Electric ice
When pieces of ice collide, small splinters break off. These have a positive electrical charge and the bigger pieces a negative charge. The small splinters are swept upwards, so they accumulate near the top of the cloud, while the bigger fragments gather near the bottom. Soon the charge is positive at the top of the cloud, and negative at the bottom.

PARTICLES FALL AFTER BEING SWEPT UP INTO THE CLOUD

LARGE ICE CRYSTALS SINK TO THE CLOUD'S BASE

THERE IS TURBULENCE WHERE UP- AND DOWN-CURRENTS MEET

THE LOWER PART OF THE CLOUD HAS A NEGATIVE CHARGE

COLD AIR SINKS DOWN

Three strokes in a flash
A lightning flash begins with a spark from the cloud to the ground, along a jagged, irregular path (1). Before it reaches the ground, this meets a return stroke, from the ground to the cloud along the same path (2). This is the main part of the flash. Then there is a new stroke from higher in the cloud (3). There are three or four strokes in a complete flash.

Hurricanes

A HURRICANE is the biggest and most violent of storms on Earth. It can be 900 kilometres across. The wind speed near the centre is always more than 120 kph (kilometres per hour), but can be more than 240 kph. Hurricanes form over the tropical oceans, between about 190 and 775 kilometres north or south of the equator. The sea temperature must be at least 27 °C and there must be a disturbance in the flow of air to set it turning.

A hurricane begins to form as warm, moist air rises rapidly and huge storm clouds grow as its moisture condenses. Once the mass of warm air starts turning, air that is drawn into the base of the clouds spirals upwards. A hurricane usually begins on the eastern side of an ocean and travels westward. Then it curves along a track that takes it away from the equator.

Inside a hurricane
Spiralling air produces a central ring of cloud with a cloud-free centre, called the eye. Beyond this lies a circle fairly clear of cloud (where the air is sinking), then a more cloudy circle (where the air is rising). The pattern is repeated outwards, but with the clouds becoming more scattered further away from the centre.

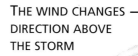

THE WIND CHANGES DIRECTION ABOVE THE STORM

Storm surge
The low pressure at the centre of a hurricane causes the sea level to rise, and the fierce winds produce big waves. When the storm reaches a coast, these combine to carry water inland, sometimes for several kilometres. The biggest hurricanes can raise the sea to more than 15 metres above its normal level. This is a storm surge.

AS WELL AS THE WIND, A HURRICANE BRINGS PROLONGED AND TORRENTIAL RAIN

THERE ARE HUGE WAVES

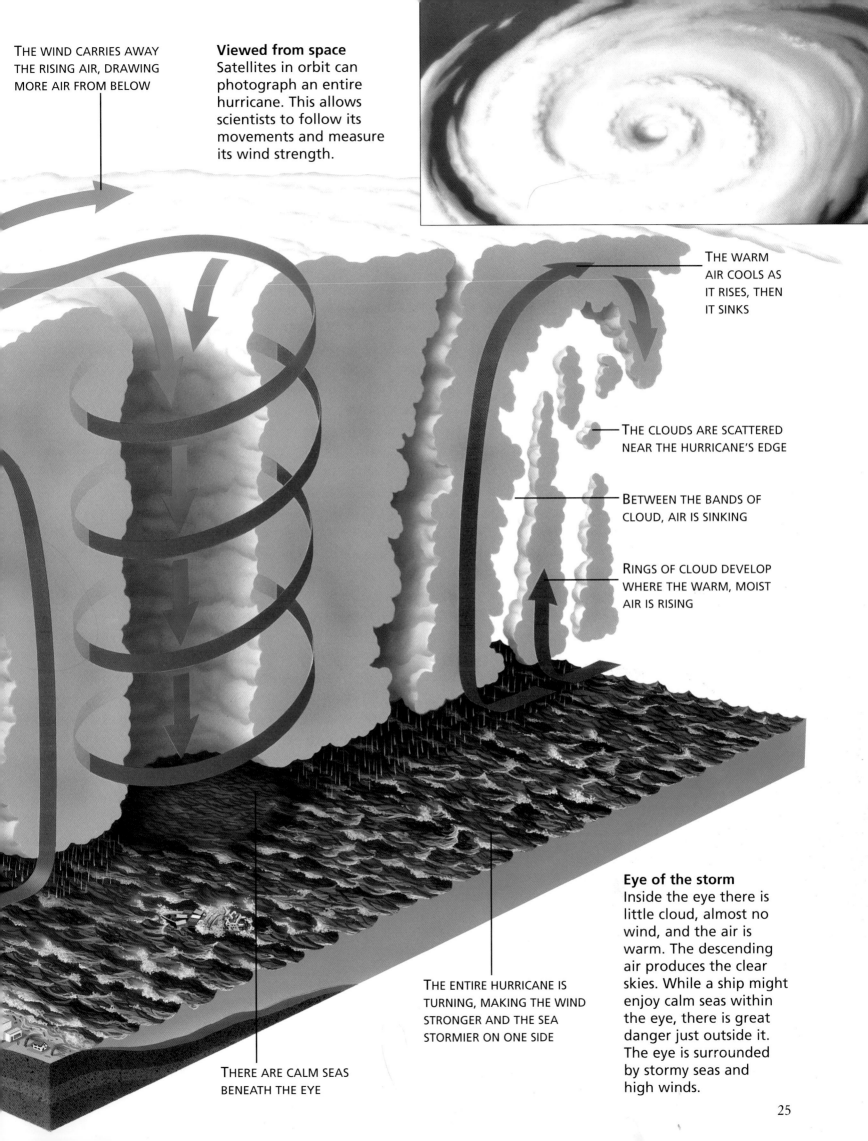

THE WIND CARRIES AWAY THE RISING AIR, DRAWING MORE AIR FROM BELOW

Viewed from space
Satellites in orbit can photograph an entire hurricane. This allows scientists to follow its movements and measure its wind strength.

THE WARM AIR COOLS AS IT RISES, THEN IT SINKS

THE CLOUDS ARE SCATTERED NEAR THE HURRICANE'S EDGE

BETWEEN THE BANDS OF CLOUD, AIR IS SINKING

RINGS OF CLOUD DEVELOP WHERE THE WARM, MOIST AIR IS RISING

Eye of the storm
Inside the eye there is little cloud, almost no wind, and the air is warm. The descending air produces the clear skies. While a ship might enjoy calm seas within the eye, there is great danger just outside it. The eye is surrounded by stormy seas and high winds.

THE ENTIRE HURRICANE IS TURNING, MAKING THE WIND STRONGER AND THE SEA STORMIER ON ONE SIDE

THERE ARE CALM SEAS BENEATH THE EYE

25

Tornadoes

TORNADOES are the fiercest and most destructive of all winds. Descending from a storm cloud, a column of rotating air becomes a tornado when it touches the ground. Air is drawn into the tornado funnel and spirals upwards. This generates a wind around the centre of at least 65 kph (kilometres per hour) and occasionally up to 500 kph. Tornadoes are rarely more than about 350 metres wide at the base and many are smaller. The wider the funnel, the stronger the winds inside.

Most tornadoes follow an erratic path over the ground, travelling at 40 to 65 kph, but sometimes at up to 100 kph. Some remain stationary. Few tornadoes last longer than about twenty minutes and many disappear after one minute or less, but occasionally one survives for several hours.

INSIDE THE CLOUD, FALLING HAIL, SNOW, AND RAIN DRAG COLD AIR DOWN

AIR IS RISING AT 100 KPH OR MORE

TORRENTIAL RAIN FALLS

THE TORNADO LEAVES A NARROW TRAIL OF DESTRUCTION

OUTSIDE THE TORNADO, RAIN AND HUGE HAILSTONES OFTEN CAUSE SERIOUS DAMAGE, ESPECIALLY TO FARM CROPS

Life of a tornado
A tornado is born when the centre of a huge storm cloud starts to rotate. This section then extends downwards until it sticks out beneath the cloud as a wall cloud (1). Part of the wall cloud then grows downwards, forming a funnel of twisting air that becomes a tornado when it touches the ground (2). Dust and debris drawn into the funnel darken it (3). Outside the funnel, the tornado throws out debris at high speed. Once the tornado lifts from the ground it is harmless (4), but it could touch down again.

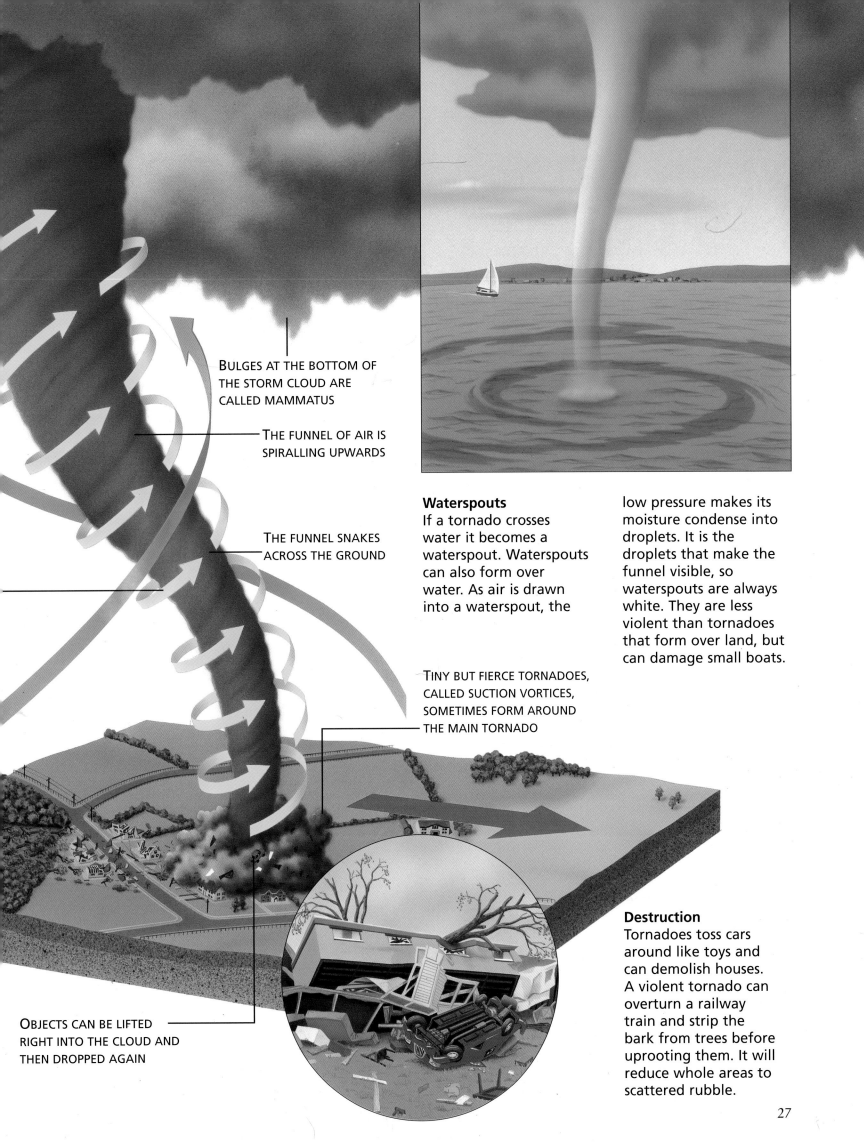

BULGES AT THE BOTTOM OF THE STORM CLOUD ARE CALLED MAMMATUS

THE FUNNEL OF AIR IS SPIRALLING UPWARDS

THE FUNNEL SNAKES ACROSS THE GROUND

TINY BUT FIERCE TORNADOES, CALLED SUCTION VORTICES, SOMETIMES FORM AROUND THE MAIN TORNADO

OBJECTS CAN BE LIFTED RIGHT INTO THE CLOUD AND THEN DROPPED AGAIN

Waterspouts

If a tornado crosses water it becomes a waterspout. Waterspouts can also form over water. As air is drawn into a waterspout, the low pressure makes its moisture condense into droplets. It is the droplets that make the funnel visible, so waterspouts are always white. They are less violent than tornadoes that form over land, but can damage small boats.

Destruction

Tornadoes toss cars around like toys and can demolish houses. A violent tornado can overturn a railway train and strip the bark from trees before uprooting them. It will reduce whole areas to scattered rubble.

27

Wind and Water

AIR MOVING away from the equator carries warmth into the far north and south, spreading the heat more evenly. This movement also produces winds near the Earth's surface. Over the oceans, the winds push the seawater. Moving water, driven by the wind, forms ocean currents.

Warm equatorial currents flow from east to west on either side of the equator in the Pacific, Atlantic, and Indian oceans. These surface currents are driven by the trade winds, which blow from the northeast in the northern hemisphere and the southeast in the southern hemisphere. In the Pacific Ocean the winds sometimes change and become weaker or stronger, or even reverse and blow in the opposite direction. This can seriously affect the weather along the Pacific coastlines.

La Niña
Sometimes the Pacific trade winds strengthen and the warm Equatorial Current moves faster. This is called La Niña. It causes very dry weather in South America and heavy rainstorms in Indonesia.

DURING LA NIÑA, STORM CLOUDS GATHER OFF THE COAST OF INDONESIA

THE TRADE WINDS, WHICH DRIVE WARM SURFACE WATER WESTWARDS

THE CIRCULATING AIR FLOWS BACK AT HIGH LEVEL

REVERSED TRADE WINDS BRING DRY WEATHER TO INDONESIA AND AUSTRALIA

THE TRADE WINDS USUALLY DRIVE THE EQUATORIAL CURRENTS IN AN EAST TO WEST DIRECTION

THE BENGUELA CURRENT CHILLS AIR CROSSING IT, PRODUCING THE DRY CLIMATE OF THE NAMIB DESERT

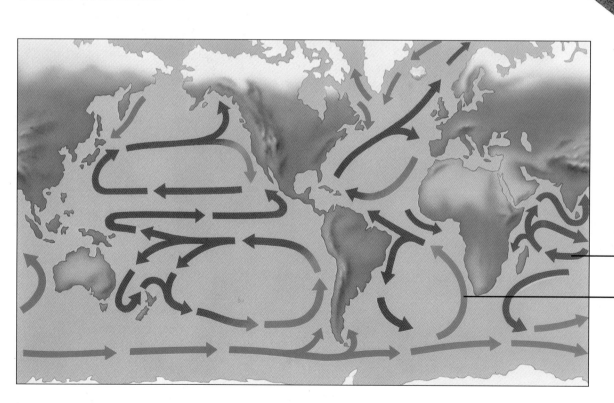

Ocean currents
In each of the oceans, the currents flow roughly in a circle, called a gyre. Warm currents (red arrows, *above*) and cold currents (blue arrows) affect the temperatures and the weather in coastal areas. For example, the cold Benguela Current affects the climate of the Namib Desert in southern Africa.

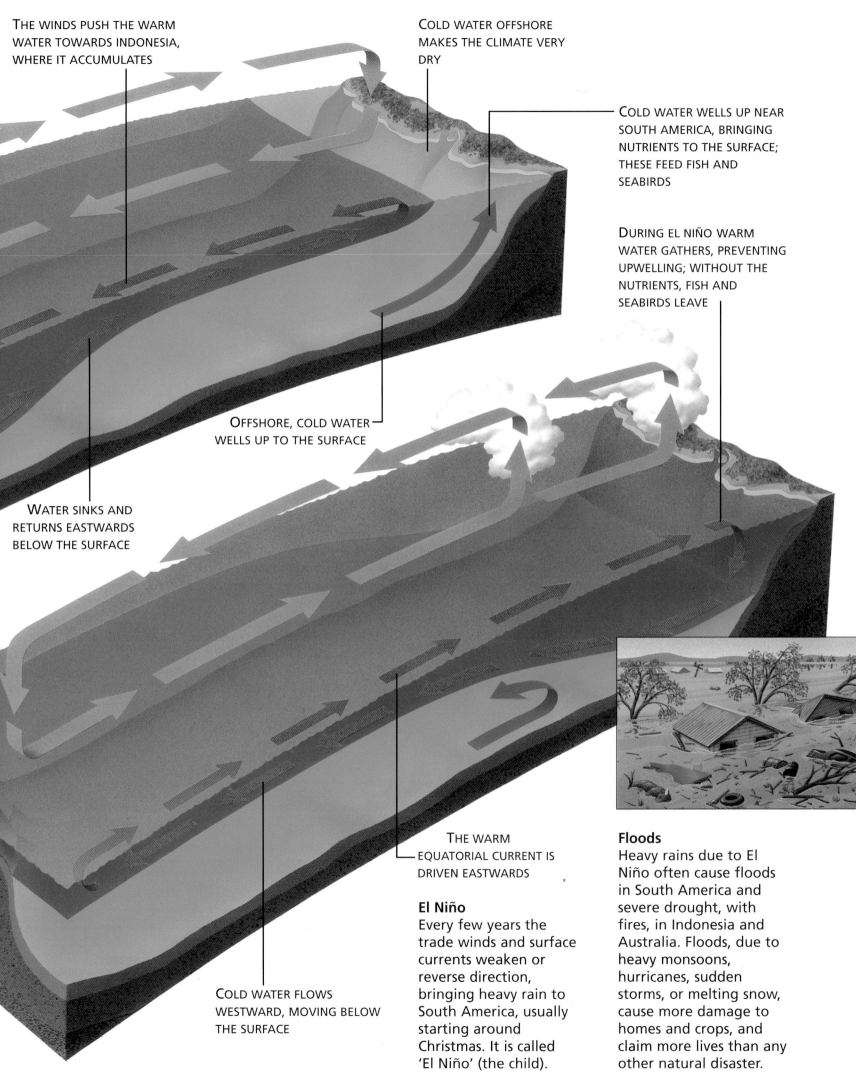

THE WINDS PUSH THE WARM WATER TOWARDS INDONESIA, WHERE IT ACCUMULATES

COLD WATER OFFSHORE MAKES THE CLIMATE VERY DRY

COLD WATER WELLS UP NEAR SOUTH AMERICA, BRINGING NUTRIENTS TO THE SURFACE; THESE FEED FISH AND SEABIRDS

DURING EL NIÑO WARM WATER GATHERS, PREVENTING UPWELLING; WITHOUT THE NUTRIENTS, FISH AND SEABIRDS LEAVE

OFFSHORE, COLD WATER WELLS UP TO THE SURFACE

WATER SINKS AND RETURNS EASTWARDS BELOW THE SURFACE

THE WARM EQUATORIAL CURRENT IS DRIVEN EASTWARDS

COLD WATER FLOWS WESTWARD, MOVING BELOW THE SURFACE

El Niño
Every few years the trade winds and surface currents weaken or reverse direction, bringing heavy rain to South America, usually starting around Christmas. It is called 'El Niño' (the child).

Floods
Heavy rains due to El Niño often cause floods in South America and severe drought, with fires, in Indonesia and Australia. Floods, due to heavy monsoons, hurricanes, sudden storms, or melting snow, cause more damage to homes and crops, and claim more lives than any other natural disaster.

29

Measuring

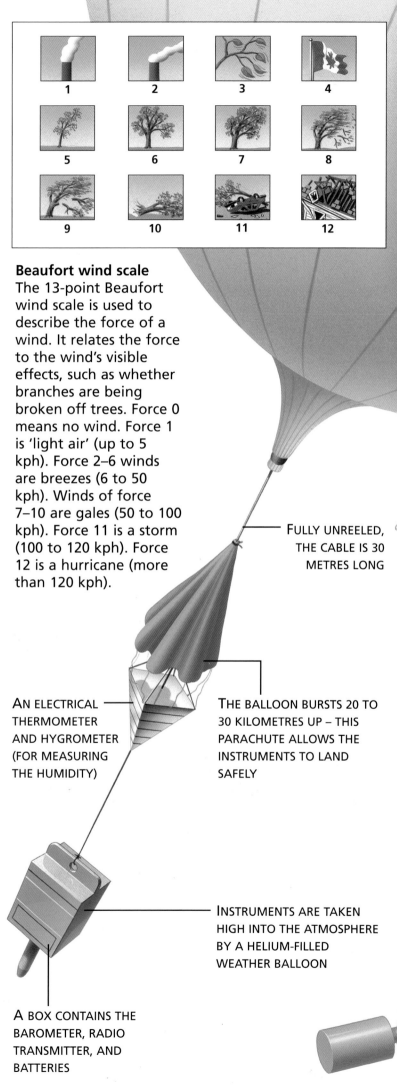

PEOPLE have always needed to forecast the weather, but until modern times they had very little to help them. They could watch the skies and see, for example, how the cirrus cloud called mares' tails often meant strong winds were on their way, and how the day after a red sunset was usually fine. They noticed how the direction of the wind was linked to whether the wind brought warm or cold, wet or dry air. They also relied on signs from plants and animals.

These indicators were not very reliable. Today, we can do much better because we have instruments to measure temperature, pressure, humidity, wind speed and direction, rainfall, and sunshine brightness. We can take these measurements not only at ground level from weather stations all over the world, but also at various heights throughout the atmosphere.

Beaufort wind scale
The 13-point Beaufort wind scale is used to describe the force of a wind. It relates the force to the wind's visible effects, such as whether branches are being broken off trees. Force 0 means no wind. Force 1 is 'light air' (up to 5 kph). Force 2–6 winds are breezes (6 to 50 kph). Winds of force 7–10 are gales (50 to 100 kph). Force 11 is a storm (100 to 120 kph). Force 12 is a hurricane (more than 120 kph).

FULLY UNREELED, THE CABLE IS 30 METRES LONG

AN ELECTRICAL THERMOMETER AND HYGROMETER (FOR MEASURING THE HUMIDITY)

THE BALLOON BURSTS 20 TO 30 KILOMETRES UP – THIS PARACHUTE ALLOWS THE INSTRUMENTS TO LAND SAFELY

INSTRUMENTS ARE TAKEN HIGH INTO THE ATMOSPHERE BY A HELIUM-FILLED WEATHER BALLOON

A BOX CONTAINS THE BAROMETER, RADIO TRANSMITTER, AND BATTERIES

Natural indicators
Some plants respond to weather conditions. Pine cones open in dry weather and close when the air is moist. Seaweed is dry and brittle when the air is dry, but absorbs water from the air and becomes soft when the air is moist. Scarlet pimpernel and morning glory are wild flowers that open when it is sunny and close when the sky is cloudy. However, natural indicators such as these show only the present weather conditions. Forecasts based on them are unreliable, because those conditions can change.

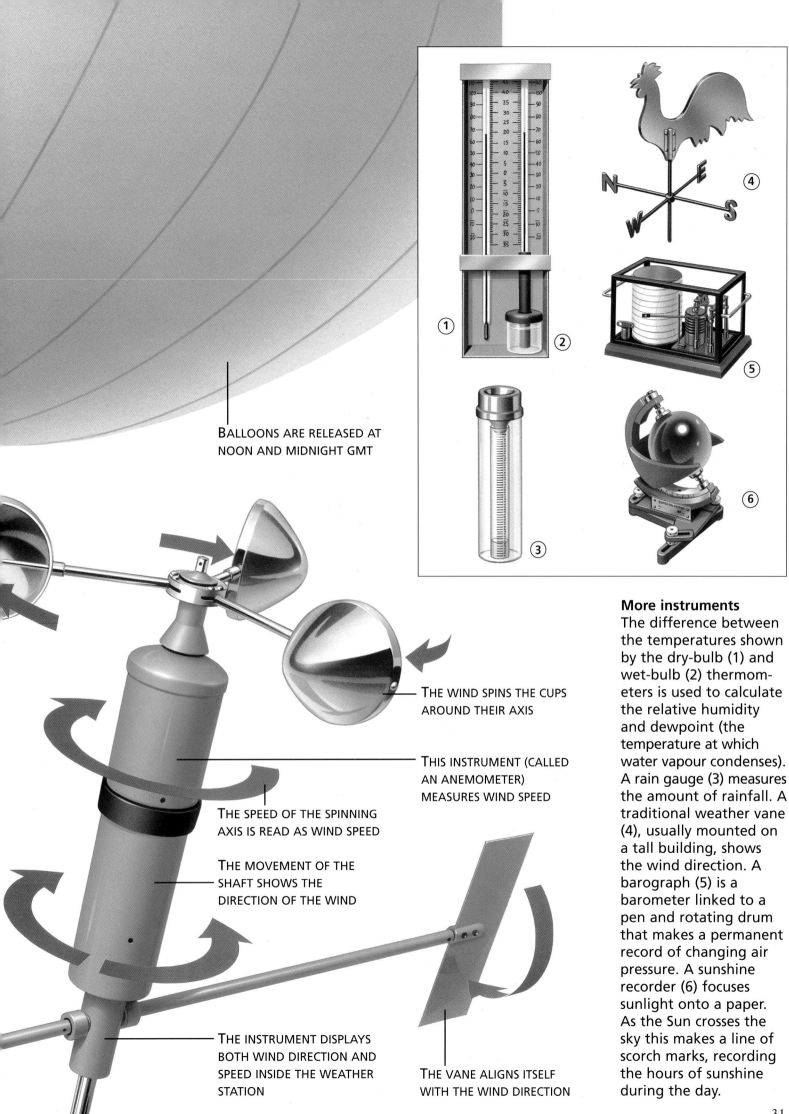

BALLOONS ARE RELEASED AT
NOON AND MIDNIGHT GMT

THE WIND SPINS THE CUPS
AROUND THEIR AXIS

THIS INSTRUMENT (CALLED
AN ANEMOMETER)
MEASURES WIND SPEED

THE SPEED OF THE SPINNING
AXIS IS READ AS WIND SPEED

THE MOVEMENT OF THE
SHAFT SHOWS THE
DIRECTION OF THE WIND

THE INSTRUMENT DISPLAYS
BOTH WIND DIRECTION AND
SPEED INSIDE THE WEATHER
STATION

THE VANE ALIGNS ITSELF
WITH THE WIND DIRECTION

More instruments
The difference between
the temperatures shown
by the dry-bulb (1) and
wet-bulb (2) thermom-
eters is used to calculate
the relative humidity
and dewpoint (the
temperature at which
water vapour condenses).
A rain gauge (3) measures
the amount of rainfall. A
traditional weather vane
(4), usually mounted on
a tall building, shows
the wind direction. A
barograph (5) is a
barometer linked to a
pen and rotating drum
that makes a permanent
record of changing air
pressure. A sunshine
recorder (6) focuses
sunlight onto a paper.
As the Sun crosses the
sky this makes a line of
scorch marks, recording
the hours of sunshine
during the day.

31

Satellites

THE WORLD'S first weather satellite was launched into orbit on 1 April 1960. It was called TIROS and was launched by the United States. Later models were called NOAA-class satellites. These satellites are in polar orbits. Each one can see a strip of the Earth's surface 3000 kilometres wide and passes over the entire surface of the Earth in 24 hours.

Today, there are many weather satellites orbiting the Earth. Between them they monitor the whole of the atmosphere all the time, transmitting their measurements and pictures to receiving stations in several countries. Satellites measure temperatures, winds, the area covered by ice, and changes in surface vegetation. This information helps scientists learn about the weather and its effects.

Geostationary orbit
A satellite travelling at 11,300 kph (kilometres per hour) at a height of 36,000 kilometres takes exactly 24 hours to complete each orbit. This is the time it takes the Earth to complete one revolution, so the satellite remains above the same position on the surface. It is then in a geostationary orbit.

Between them, five weather satellites in equatorial geostationary orbit monitor the entire surface of the Earth.

THE RADIOMETER MEASURES VISIBLE AND INFRARED RADIATION

SOLAR PANELS GENERATE ELECTRICITY FROM SUNLIGHT TO SUPPLY POWER FOR THE EQUIPMENT

Meteosat
Meteosat was built and launched by the European Space Agency into geostationary orbit over the equator at 0° longitude. The satellite is 3.2 metres long and 2.1 metres wide. It spins at 100 revolutions per minute and lies on its side, with its 'nose' pointing north.

ONE OF THE FOUR VHF RADIO COMMUNICATIONS ANTENNAE

INFORMATION IS RADIOED TO BASE IN DARMSTADT, GERMANY

MORE RADIO ANTENNAE ARE HOUSED INSIDE THIS CASING

ONE OF THE TRANSMITTING ANTENNAE AROUND THE OUTSIDE OF THE COMMUNICATIONS UNIT

THIS UNIT SENDS SIGNALS TO THE VHF ANTENNAE

A PLATFORM CARRIES THE RADIOMETER, OTHER INSTRUMENTS, AND THE FUEL TANK FOR THE ROCKET ENGINE

SATELLITES IN GEOSTATIONARY ORBIT ARE OVER THE EQUATOR

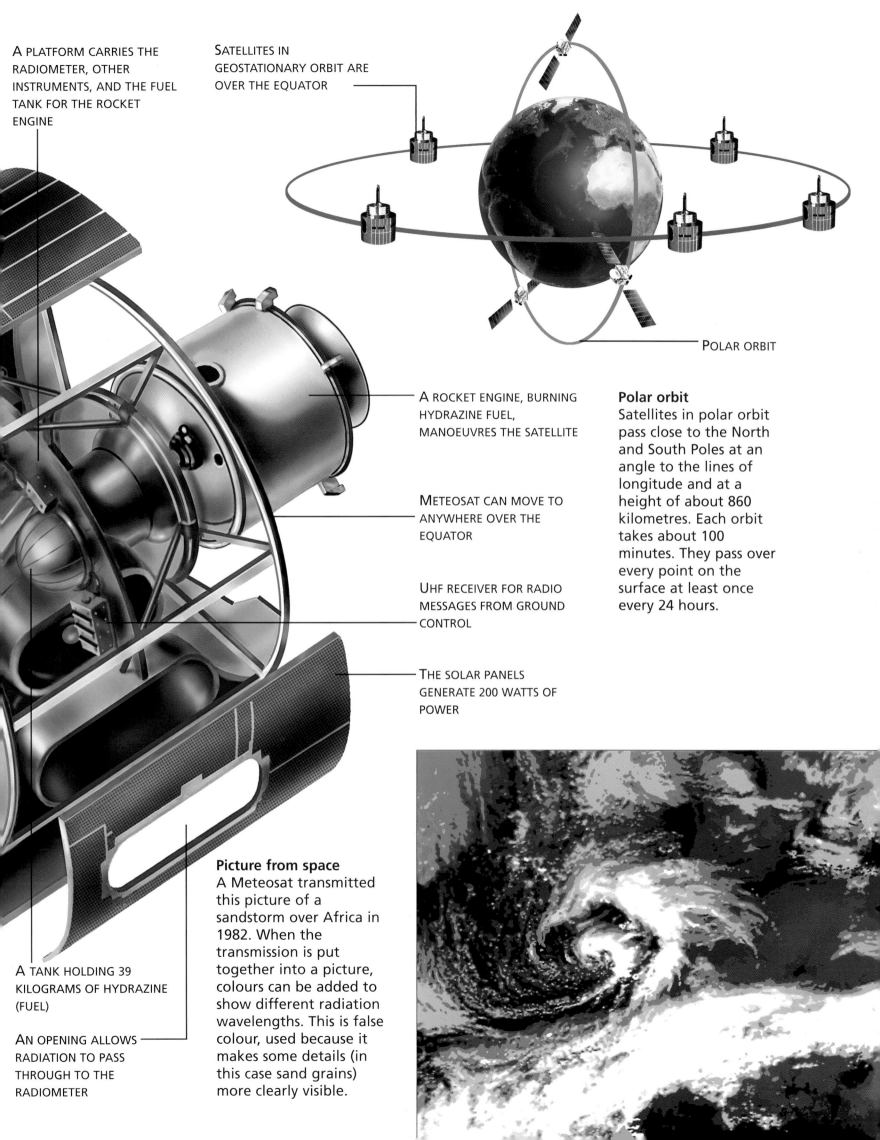

POLAR ORBIT

A ROCKET ENGINE, BURNING HYDRAZINE FUEL, MANOEUVRES THE SATELLITE

METEOSAT CAN MOVE TO ANYWHERE OVER THE EQUATOR

UHF RECEIVER FOR RADIO MESSAGES FROM GROUND CONTROL

THE SOLAR PANELS GENERATE 200 WATTS OF POWER

Polar orbit
Satellites in polar orbit pass close to the North and South Poles at an angle to the lines of longitude and at a height of about 860 kilometres. Each orbit takes about 100 minutes. They pass over every point on the surface at least once every 24 hours.

A TANK HOLDING 39 KILOGRAMS OF HYDRAZINE (FUEL)

AN OPENING ALLOWS RADIATION TO PASS THROUGH TO THE RADIOMETER

Picture from space
A Meteosat transmitted this picture of a sandstorm over Africa in 1982. When the transmission is put together into a picture, colours can be added to show different radiation wavelengths. This is false colour, used because it makes some details (in this case sand grains) more clearly visible.

Forecasts

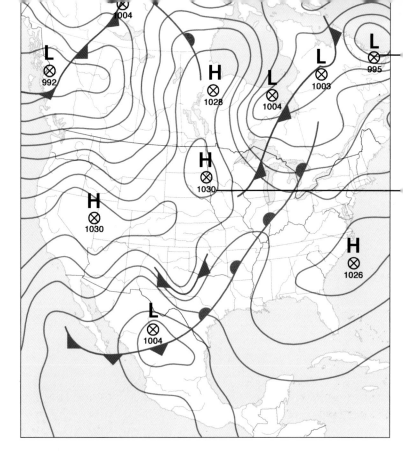

WEATHER forecasts shown on television last for only a few minutes – long enough for the presenter to tell viewers whether it will be sunny or cloudy, fine or wet, and whether to expect strong winds, flooding, snow or ice. Radio carries more detailed forecasts for people such as farmers and fishermen. Airports, military or civilian, employ professional meteorologists to compile aviation forecasts.

A forecast is based on data sent from thousands of weather stations on land and at sea, from ships and buoys, and aircraft on routine flights. Specialized weather aircraft send details of individual weather systems, and satellites in orbit high above the Earth transmit a constant stream of measurements.

Synoptic chart
Meteorologists prepare synoptic charts to show weather conditions over a large area. The lines are isobars, joining places where surface air pressure is the same. Centres of high and low pressure are marked. Warm and cold weather fronts cross the isobars. The chart is updated every few hours to show where and how fast the weather is moving.

TV weather forecast
A TV forecast gives an outline of weather conditions over a large area for about the next 24 hours. It may also provide a more general forecast for up to about three days. It is not possible to forecast what the weather will be like more than about a week in advance.

A professional meteorologist prepares the forecast and may present it, but the presenter is often a non-expert reading a script.

SATELLITE PICTURES OF CLOUD TYPES AND PATTERNS SHOW THE MOVEMENT OF WEATHER

SOLAR CELLS GENERATE POWER FOR THE SATELLITE EQUIPMENT

STANDARD SYMBOLS SHOW SUNSHINE, CLOUD, SHOWERS, OR CONTINUOUS RAIN

SHIPS RADIO MEASUREMENTS OF AIR AND SEA-SURFACE TEMPERATURE, AND OTHER WEATHER CONDITIONS TO A FORECASTING CENTRE

— SYMBOLS INDICATE THE LOCATION OF WEATHER STATIONS

— THE REPORTED AIR PRESSURE IN MILLIBARS IS SHOWN FOR EACH WEATHER STATION

Recording the weather
Weather satellites (1, 2) can measure air and sea temperatures, and cloud, snow and ice cover. They can even measure the height of waves on the sea. They transmit the information to surface receiving stations (3) where it is used in preparing forecasts and for research. The other information that is radioed, faxed, or emailed to weather stations come from numerous sources. Weather balloons (4) are sent up from hundreds of places around the world every day to collect data from high in the atmosphere. Aircraft fitted with sensitive instruments and radar (5), measure conditions inside weather systems, such as depressions. Many instruments are used in ground level stations (see *pages 30–31*). The instruments are often housed in a special box called a Stevenson screen (6).

WEATHER BUOYS AT SEA REPORT WEATHER CONDITIONS AUTOMATICALLY

Pollution

A N AIRBORNE substance that can harm people or other living organisms is called a pollutant. It may be in the form of a gas, liquid particles, or solid particles. The wind and rain can carry pollutants many kilometres from their source. Certain weather conditions, such as intense sunshine and temperature inversion (see *right*) can make pollution worse in our cities.

Some pollutants occur naturally (for example, volcanoes eject gases and ash). We can do nothing about these, but we can try to reduce the pollution we cause ourselves. Many industrial processes produce substances that can pollute the air. We can trap them before they escape. Car exhausts also cause pollution. We can reduce this by making engines more efficient and by trapping pollutants with catalytic converters.

City pollution

Pollution is usually worst over cities, where there are more sources of pollution. The pollutants cannot disperse if there is a temperature inversion. Instead of the air being warmer near the ground and cooler higher up, the opposite occurs. This can hold pollution over a city for days.

SOMETIMES WARM AIR LIES ABOVE COOLER AIR AND A DOME FORMS

COOL AIR MOVES IN FROM THE NEARBY COUNTRYSIDE

A LAYER OF WARM AIR TRAPS A LAYER OF COLD AIR BELOW IT

POLLUTANTS ARE TRAPPED BENEATH THE DOME AND ACCUMULATE

Acid rain

Burning some kinds of coal and oil releases sulphur dioxide and nitrogen oxides. These gases can be carried a long way by the wind. While they are airborne, they react with oxygen and water, and eventually form tiny droplets of sulphuric and nitric acid that dissolve in cloud droplets or stick to solids. This pollution is called acid rain. It can harm plants and make lakes and rivers acidic.

Cement dust

Cement-making involves crushing and grinding rock into fine powder. This can release minute dust particles into the air. Cement dust makes people cough and wheeze, especially if they have asthma, and can cause bronchitis. Its release is strictly controlled in most parts of the world.

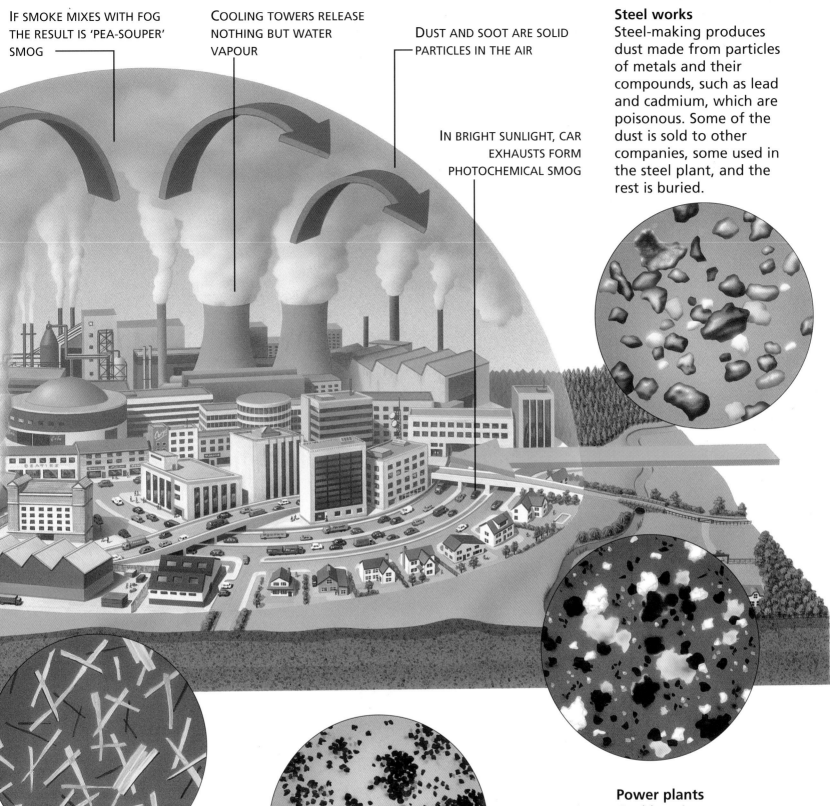

IF SMOKE MIXES WITH FOG THE RESULT IS 'PEA-SOUPER' SMOG

COOLING TOWERS RELEASE NOTHING BUT WATER VAPOUR

DUST AND SOOT ARE SOLID PARTICLES IN THE AIR

IN BRIGHT SUNLIGHT, CAR EXHAUSTS FORM PHOTOCHEMICAL SMOG

Steel works

Steel-making produces dust made from particles of metals and their compounds, such as lead and cadmium, which are poisonous. Some of the dust is sold to other companies, some used in the steel plant, and the rest is buried.

Asbestos

Asbestos is a mineral made from fibrous particles. It was once used for fireproofing and to make roofs and brake linings. Inhaling the fibres can cause serious lung damage. Its use is now banned in most countries.

Car exhaust

As well as gases, car exhausts emit small particles of unburned fuel. Inhaling these can damage the lungs. In strong sunlight they react with exhaust gases to form photochemical smog that is also harmful to health.

Power plants

Coal-burning power plants produce ash as a waste product. Called fly ash, it consists of very fine grains of a variety of minerals. It can be harmful if inhaled, but it has a number of industrial uses, so is collected.

Global Warming

SUNLIGHT passes straight through the air, all the way to the Earth's surface. It warms the land and sea surface and when these are warmed, they radiate heat. Certain gases that are naturally present in the atmosphere absorb, and so trap, some of this outgoing heat. This is called the greenhouse effect and without it the world would be very much colder than it is. The gases that absorb the heat include water vapour, carbon dioxide, methane, ozone, and nitrous oxide. We are now adding to the quantities of some of these greenhouse gases. Scientists have calculated how much heat the extra amounts are likely to absorb. The heat is expected to raise the average temperature of climates throughout the world. This is global warming. How much warming there will be and its effect in different regions remain uncertain.

Sunlight
The Sun radiates light and heat. Its strongest radiation is at the short wavelengths we see as visible light. This radiation passes through the air, but is reflected from cloud tops.

CLOUDS MAKE NIGHTS WARMER, DAYS COOLER

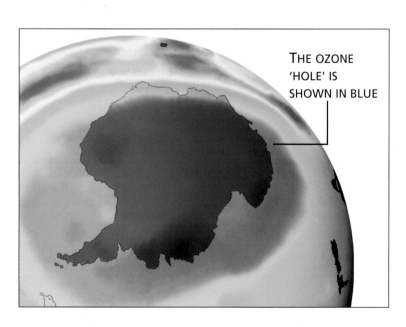

THE OZONE 'HOLE' IS SHOWN IN BLUE

Ozone 'hole'
Ultraviolet radiation from the Sun can cause skin cancer. The ozone gas layer in the strato-sphere protects us by absorbing some of the radiation. Chemicals in spray cans, fridges, and air conditioners reduce the amount of ozone, mainly over Antarctica in spring. These chemicals are no longer used and the ozone layer will eventually recover.

Factories and fuel
Burning coal, oil, and gas releases carbon dioxide into the air. Factories are working to reduce the amount they release by using fuel more efficiently. Reducing waste means using less fuel. Gas releases less carbon dioxide than oil or coal.

Conventional power stations release carbon dioxide gas, but nuclear plants emit none. Oil companies are developing alternatives to petroleum to reduce greenhouse gas emissions.

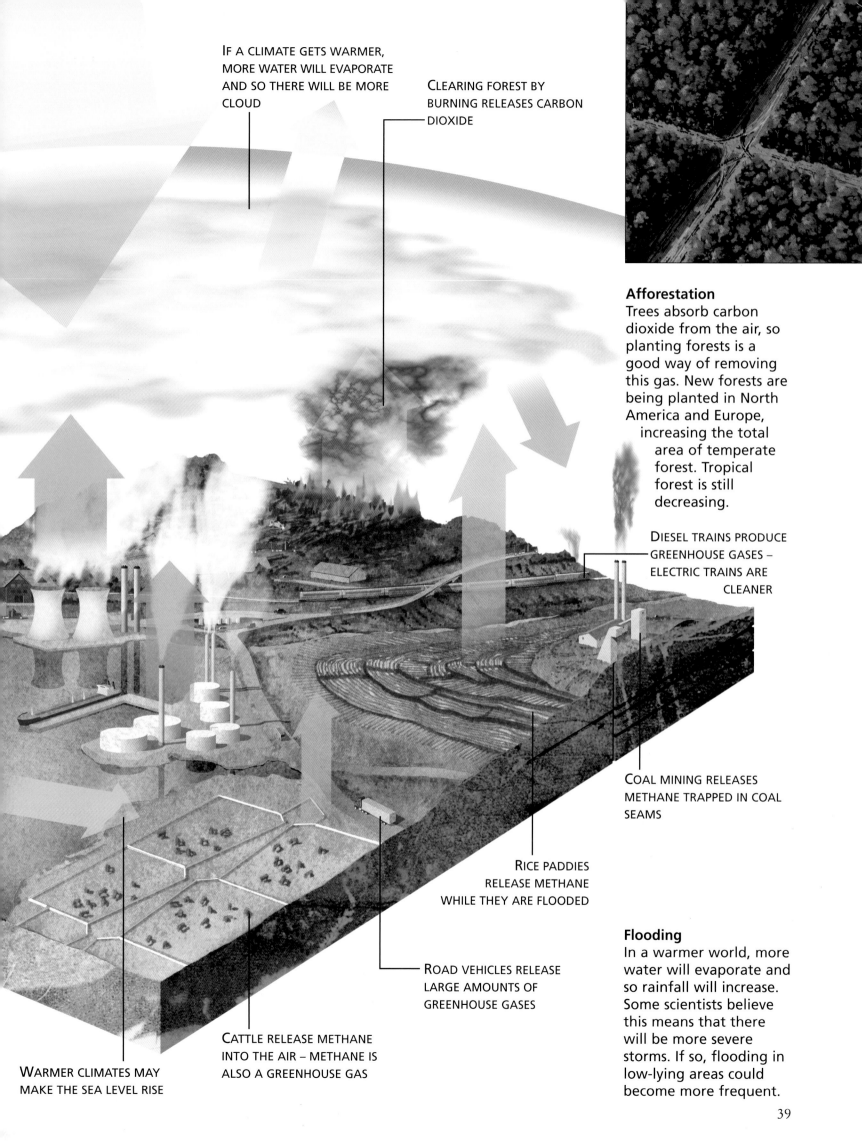

IF A CLIMATE GETS WARMER, MORE WATER WILL EVAPORATE AND SO THERE WILL BE MORE CLOUD

CLEARING FOREST BY BURNING RELEASES CARBON DIOXIDE

Afforestation
Trees absorb carbon dioxide from the air, so planting forests is a good way of removing this gas. New forests are being planted in North America and Europe, increasing the total area of temperate forest. Tropical forest is still decreasing.

DIESEL TRAINS PRODUCE GREENHOUSE GASES – ELECTRIC TRAINS ARE CLEANER

COAL MINING RELEASES METHANE TRAPPED IN COAL SEAMS

RICE PADDIES RELEASE METHANE WHILE THEY ARE FLOODED

ROAD VEHICLES RELEASE LARGE AMOUNTS OF GREENHOUSE GASES

Flooding
In a warmer world, more water will evaporate and so rainfall will increase. Some scientists believe this means that there will be more severe storms. If so, flooding in low-lying areas could become more frequent.

CATTLE RELEASE METHANE INTO THE AIR – METHANE IS ALSO A GREENHOUSE GAS

WARMER CLIMATES MAY MAKE THE SEA LEVEL RISE

Protection

THE HOUSES we live in and the clothes we wear keep us warm and dry. We can look out of the window at the rain lashing down, or the snow piling ever higher in drifts, while staying safe and comfortable. We are protected from the weather.

Rain, snow, and wind are features of ordinary weather, but the weather can be extraordinary and then we need extra protection. Snow avalanches can sweep away houses. Hurricanes can cause storm surges that send water far inland to flood homes and businesses. Rivers can overflow and heavy rain can loosen the earth, causing landslides and mudslides. A lack of rain also brings danger. Extreme heat can kill and prolonged drought can ruin farmers. Facing so much danger, it is not surprising that we have found many ways to protect ourselves from the weather.

THE SEA WEARS DOWN ROCK TO BEACH PEBBLES AND THEN SAND GRAINS

LARGE ROCKS, CALLED RIP-RAP, ABSORB THE ENERGY OF WAVES, PREVENTING EROSION

Flood plains

A river meanders slowly as it crosses fairly level ground. The area covered by the meanders is the river's flood plain. The meanders slowly advance down the plain and the river overflows after heavy rain or when snow melts in spring. As a result, the plain may flood from time to time.

DIVERTING WATER INTO RESERVOIRS PROTECTS HOUSES ON THE FLOOD PLAIN

Dams

Opening and closing a dam regulates the flow of water downstream and many dams also generate electricity. Dams prevent flooding, but the reservoir behind the dam fills a valley that may once have been inhabited.

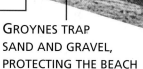

Sea defences

Storms at sea send huge waves crashing against the shore. Their power is immense. Coastal cliffs are the remains of hills, the rest of which have been washed away by the sea. It is not always possible to prevent the sea from eating away at the coast, but some stretches can be protected. Sea walls (1) and loose rocks (2) absorb wave energy. Groynes (3) trap beach material. A closed barrage (4) will hold back a storm surge.

A STORM SURGE CAN FLOOD THE LAND

GROYNES TRAP SAND AND GRAVEL, PROTECTING THE BEACH

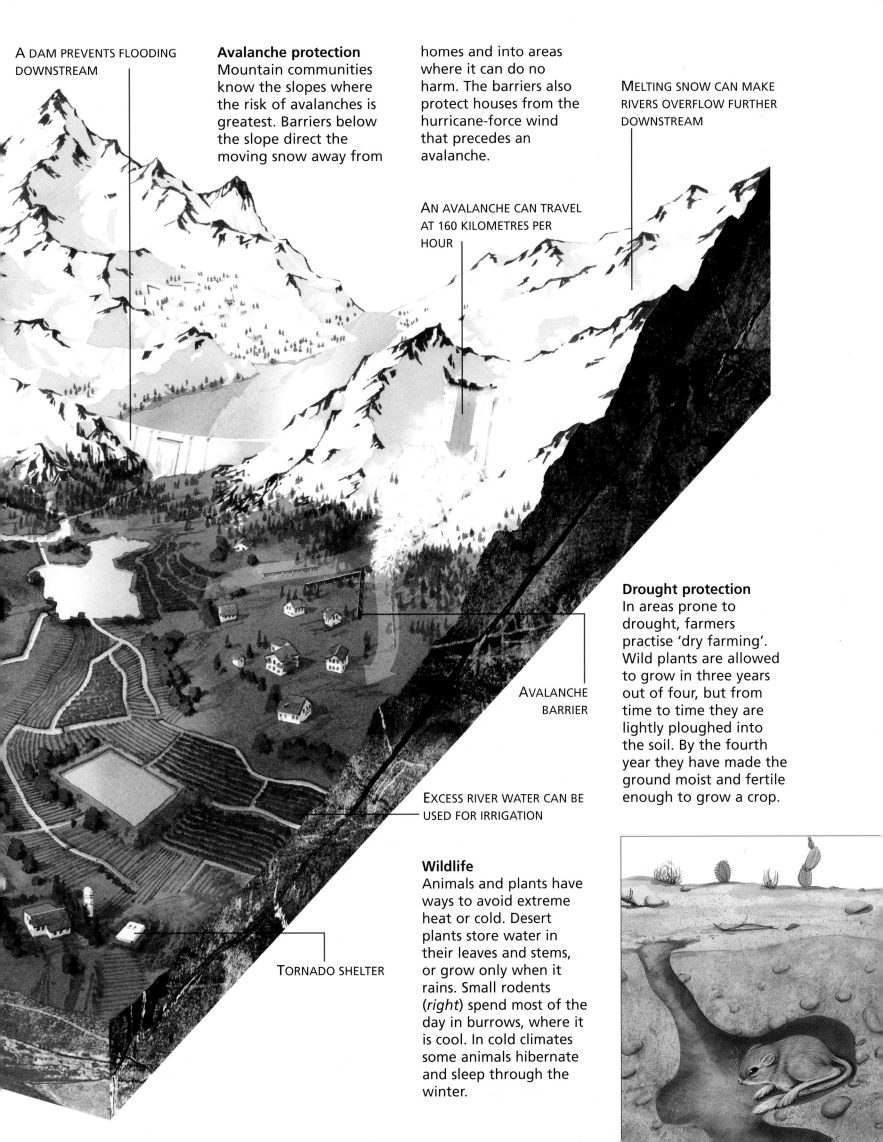

A DAM PREVENTS FLOODING DOWNSTREAM

Avalanche protection
Mountain communities know the slopes where the risk of avalanches is greatest. Barriers below the slope direct the moving snow away from homes and into areas where it can do no harm. The barriers also protect houses from the hurricane-force wind that precedes an avalanche.

MELTING SNOW CAN MAKE RIVERS OVERFLOW FURTHER DOWNSTREAM

AN AVALANCHE CAN TRAVEL AT 160 KILOMETRES PER HOUR

AVALANCHE BARRIER

EXCESS RIVER WATER CAN BE USED FOR IRRIGATION

Drought protection
In areas prone to drought, farmers practise 'dry farming'. Wild plants are allowed to grow in three years out of four, but from time to time they are lightly ploughed into the soil. By the fourth year they have made the ground moist and fertile enough to grow a crop.

Wildlife
Animals and plants have ways to avoid extreme heat or cold. Desert plants store water in their leaves and stems, or grow only when it rains. Small rodents (*right*) spend most of the day in burrows, where it is cool. In cold climates some animals hibernate and sleep through the winter.

TORNADO SHELTER

Weather Power

THE SUN radiates a huge amount of energy. This energy produces our weather. Energy from the Sun (solar energy) can also provide heating and be converted into electricity.

Many houses have solar panels on the roof. These use the warmth of sunshine to heat water, reducing fuel bills. Solar ponds concentrate enough heat for industrial use. Some buildings are equipped with solar cells, which convert sunlight into electricity. In years to come, if the cost of generating electricity this way falls, solar cells will be more widely used.

Sunlight focused on a very large scale can run a power station. Wind is part of the weather, so it is also caused by sunshine. It, too, can generate electricity. Wind turbines are a familiar sight, but wind energy might be captured on a much bigger scale.

A TORNADO'S POWER COULD BE USED TO SPIN A TURBINE

Solar station
An array of mirrors focuses the sunlight onto a furnace near the top of a tower. Sodium is heated as it is piped through the furnace. The hot sodium is then used to boil water.

TO BE USABLE, SOLAR ENERGY MUST BE FOCUSED

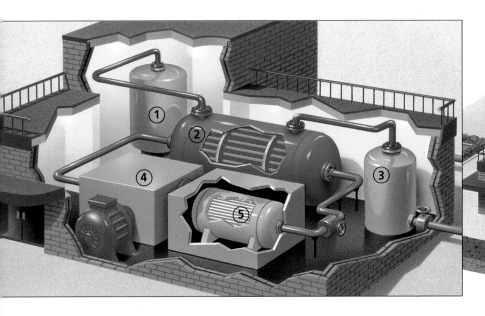

Solar generator
Hot sodium (1) passes through a heat exchanger (2) where it vaporizes water. Now cold (3), the sodium returns to the tower, where focused sunlight heats it again. Steam from the heat exchanger spins a turbine (4) to generate electricity. The steam then passes through a condenser (5) to be converted back into water before returning to the heat exchanger.

A FULL-SCALE SOLAR STATION CAN PRODUCE ONE-TENTH OF THE POWER OF A LARGE COAL, GAS, OR NUCLEAR POWER STATION

THERE ARE HUNDREDS OF PANELS, EACH WITH SEVERAL MIRRORS FOCUSING THE SUNLIGHT

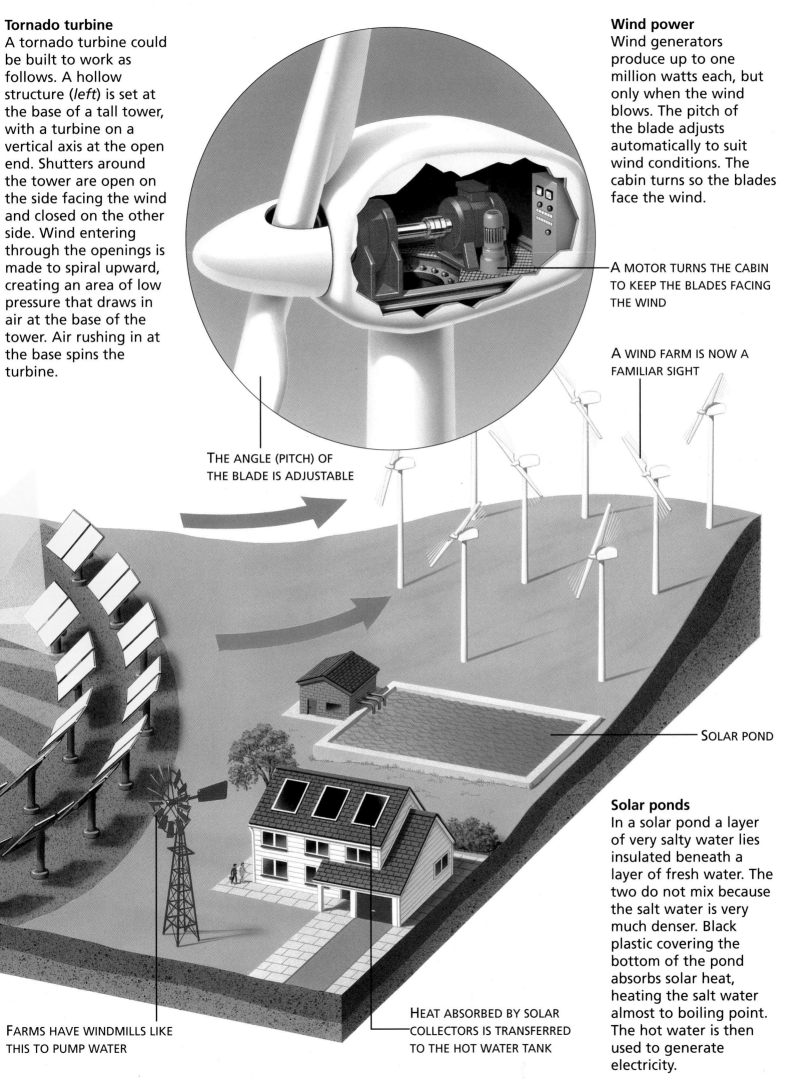

Tornado turbine

A tornado turbine could be built to work as follows. A hollow structure (*left*) is set at the base of a tall tower, with a turbine on a vertical axis at the open end. Shutters around the tower are open on the side facing the wind and closed on the other side. Wind entering through the openings is made to spiral upward, creating an area of low pressure that draws in air at the base of the tower. Air rushing in at the base spins the turbine.

Wind power

Wind generators produce up to one million watts each, but only when the wind blows. The pitch of the blade adjusts automatically to suit wind conditions. The cabin turns so the blades face the wind.

A MOTOR TURNS THE CABIN TO KEEP THE BLADES FACING THE WIND

A WIND FARM IS NOW A FAMILIAR SIGHT

THE ANGLE (PITCH) OF THE BLADE IS ADJUSTABLE

SOLAR POND

Solar ponds

In a solar pond a layer of very salty water lies insulated beneath a layer of fresh water. The two do not mix because the salt water is very much denser. Black plastic covering the bottom of the pond absorbs solar heat, heating the salt water almost to boiling point. The hot water is then used to generate electricity.

FARMS HAVE WINDMILLS LIKE THIS TO PUMP WATER

HEAT ABSORBED BY SOLAR COLLECTORS IS TRANSFERRED TO THE HOT WATER TANK

Landscapes

WATER SEEPS into tiny cracks in a rock. In winter that water freezes. As it does so it expands, widening the crack. When the ice melts in spring, the crack is bigger. This happens every winter until the rock falls apart. The falling rock crashes into other rocks, breaking chips off them. Some of these fall into a river, which rolls and grinds them together. Winds hurl other rock fragments into solid rock. Over thousands of years they wear away.

Wind and water are constantly reshaping the landscape. Sometimes changes happen suddenly, such as in a big landslide or rock fall. But changes usually happen slowly. Movements of the Earth's crust raise mountains. The weather then wears them down until they are smooth, gently rolling hills. Finally, there is only a level plain.

Desert landscape
Wind and occasional rain producing torrents of water shape the desert surface. They wear rocks down to particles the size of sand and dust grains, then hurl these grains with great force against bigger rocks. The softer parts of the rock wear away first, leaving harder rock behind. These often form strange shapes. The loose sand is blown into dunes. The shape of dunes indicates the main wind direction.

CANYONS ARE DEEP, AND CUT BY RIVERS ENTERING FROM OUTSIDE THE DESERT

A FLAT-TOPPED HILL OR SMALL PLATEAU LIKE THIS IS CALLED A MESA

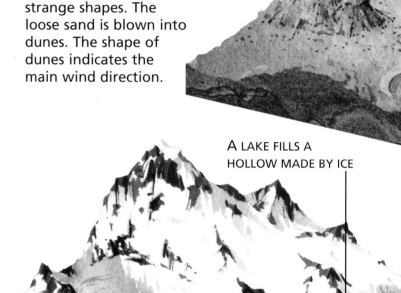

A LAKE FILLS A HOLLOW MADE BY ICE

JAGGED MOUNTAINS ARE YOUNG – IN TIME THE WEATHER WILL WEAR THEM SMOOTH

Temperate landscape
Ice sheets, thousands of metres thick, have covered much of northern Europe and North America several times over the last two million years. The immense weight of the ice makes it flow and, as it moves, it scours away all the soil and loose rock. When at last the ice melts, the landscape is bare. But the area is marked with U-shaped valleys made by glaciers, hollows that once held ice and now contain lakes, and piles of rocks, called moraines, that glaciers pushed into their present positions.

A SMALL RIVER RUNS THROUGH A LARGE U-SHAPED VALLEY THAT WAS MADE BY A GLACIER

A HANGING VALLEY, MADE BY A TRIBUTARY GLACIER, ENDS WITH A WATERFALL

THIS BEACH WAS MADE WHEN THE SEA LEVEL WAS HIGHER

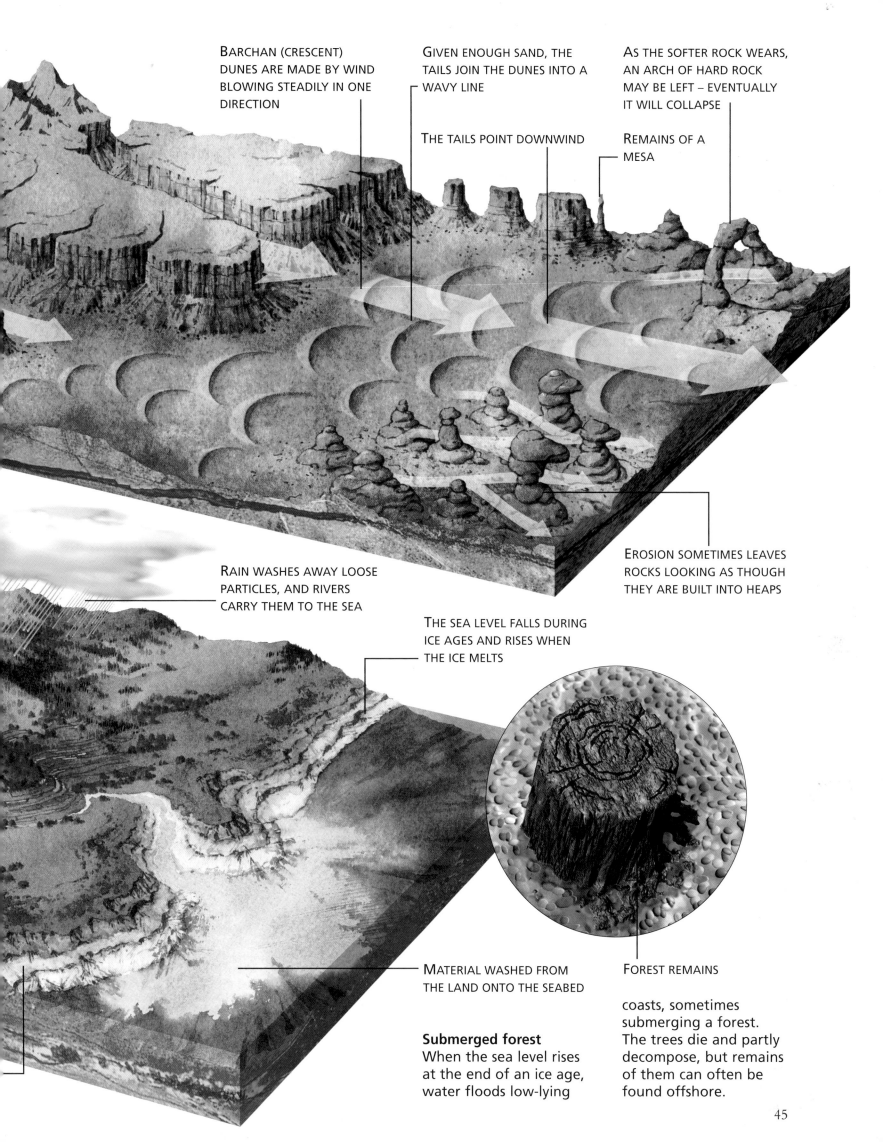

BARCHAN (CRESCENT) DUNES ARE MADE BY WIND BLOWING STEADILY IN ONE DIRECTION

GIVEN ENOUGH SAND, THE TAILS JOIN THE DUNES INTO A WAVY LINE

THE TAILS POINT DOWNWIND

AS THE SOFTER ROCK WEARS, AN ARCH OF HARD ROCK MAY BE LEFT – EVENTUALLY IT WILL COLLAPSE

REMAINS OF A MESA

EROSION SOMETIMES LEAVES ROCKS LOOKING AS THOUGH THEY ARE BUILT INTO HEAPS

RAIN WASHES AWAY LOOSE PARTICLES, AND RIVERS CARRY THEM TO THE SEA

THE SEA LEVEL FALLS DURING ICE AGES AND RISES WHEN THE ICE MELTS

MATERIAL WASHED FROM THE LAND ONTO THE SEABED

FOREST REMAINS

Submerged forest
When the sea level rises at the end of an ice age, water floods low-lying coasts, sometimes submerging a forest. The trees die and partly decompose, but remains of them can often be found offshore.

Index